FREUDIAN UNCONSCIOUS AND COGNITIVE NEUROSCIENCE

FREUDIAN UNCONSCIOUS AND COGNITIVE NEUROSCIENCE

From Unconscious Fantasies to Neural Algorithms

Vesa Talvitie

KARNAC

First published 2009 by
Karnac Books Ltd
118 Finchley Road, London NW3 5HT

Copyright © 2009 Vesa Talvitie

British Library Cataloguing in Publication Data

A C.I.P. for this book is available from the British Library

ISBN: 978 1 85575 503 1

Cover image: Ollie Samarja, *Window with Red Stripe*. www. samarja.com

Edited, designed and produced by The Studio Publishing Services Ltd,
www.publishingservicesuk.co.uk
e-mail: studio@publishingservicesuk.co.uk

Printed in Great Britain

www.karnacbooks.com

CONTENTS

ACKNOWLEDGEMENTS

I am grateful to many people for intensive discussions around the topics of this book during past years. First of all, I want to mention my supervisors, Juhani Ihanus and Hannu Tiitinen, and Olli Louhimo. Rauno Juntumaa presented valuable comments on the manuscript. I would have felt intellectual loneliness without conversations with the following brainy gentlemen: Alan T. Lloyd, Harry Schlepperman, and Fred Levin; Henrik Enckell, Jussi Kotkavirta, and Turo Reenkola; Simo Korkee and Petri Meronen. I want also thank Olli Sarmaja for the permission to use his painting as the cover image.

ABOUT THE AUTHOR

Vesa Talvitie is a Doctor of Psychology, licensed psychotherapist, and organizational consultant (FINOD). He works currently as an occupational psychologist for the City of Helsinki. He has published, in both English and Finnish, several scientific and popular articles on psychoanalytic and cognitive views of unconscious processes, neuropsychoanalysis, the nature of psychological explanations, and organizational dynamics.

Introduction

"What in man neither becomes reduced to (neuro)physical matters, nor appears in the scope of consciousness?"

Vesa Talvitie

This puzzle leads us to the core of this book: the answer from psychoanalysts would be "the (mental) unconscious", whereas cognitivists and evolutionary psychologists would use the terms "computations", or "computational level of explanation"; "evolutionary and psychic functions"; "design-level explanation" in their answers. In this book, the aim is to show that the first answer can be seen in terms of the latter answers—an approach is created through which phenomena found by psychoanalysts can be studied in the framework of cognitive science.

As a young student of psychology I had a strong dislike for the term "artificial intelligence". I had a vague idea of becoming some kind of clinical psychologist, and later I actually worked in a psychiatric hospital, a crisis unit, and a prison. I was also in personal psychoanalysis, and became a licensed psychotherapist. The dislike had something to do with a feeling that in the core of man there is something that is wholly different from machines of whatever kind. In my mind "cognitive science" was—as actually is the case—closely related to "artificial intelligence". Thus, for me, artificial intelligence cast a dark shadow on cognitive science, too.

In 1991, I had to read Howard Gardner's *Mind's New Science* for one of the last tests for the Master of Psychology degree. Gardner was able to show the origins and interests of cognitive science in such a way that the student's eyes opened. I began to devour Jerry Fodor's, Steven Stich's, the Churchlands', and Daniel Dennett's ideas on representations, neural algorithms, computation, Turing's machines, Mother Nature's intentions, and so on. In the same year, Göte Nyman, Professor of Psychology in the university of Helsinki, presented the following challenge in a debate that took place in the Finnish psychological journal: psychoanalysts should try to formulate their theoretical ideas by using the terminology of cognitive science. In my mind, Göte's statement became a simple project of translation from the psychoanalytic terminology to that of cognitive science: just take a phenomena found by psychoanalysts, read some cognitivists' books, and pick the best explanation for the "Freudian" phenomenon.

I still think that humans are not machines. After having read Gardner's book, however, that conviction has not prevented me from becoming fascinated with the perspectives introduced by a cognitive orientation. On this basis, I welcome especially those readers who possess prejudices towards either psychoanalysis or cognitive science: I have had (and still have) them both. One might say that this book is made as a result of them.

The "Freudian" thing I grasped in my project of translation was the unconscious. The role of it in psychoanalytic thinking cannot be overemphasized—it is the "cornerstone" without which psychoanalysis would lack its characteristics. The idea of repression, for instance, makes sense only through the term "unconscious", and the term "transference" is also grounded in it. The unconscious is not a theoretical concept existing just in the theoretical realm, but has practical effects upon clinical psychoanalysis: psychoanalysts' work is directed by the principle that the aim of the psychoanalytic cure is to make the unconscious (repressed) conscious. All in all, without the unconscious, there would be no such a thing as psychoanalysis.

For decades, psychoanalysis has had a monopoly on the unconscious. From the 1970s onwards, however, the cognitive orientation has studied it in the scope of several empirical settings and under a variety of concepts: at the very least, one must mention the terms "implicit memory", "implicit knowledge", "procedural knowledge", "semantic activation without conscious identification", and "tacit knowledge". We can even say that after the cognitive orientation—or cognitive science—had become interested in consciousness, there was a boom in the study of the unconscious.

Moreover, in the scope of evolutionary theory, perspectives have emerged that are more than closely related to the Freudian unconscious. First, in the 1970s, Robert Trivers published his classic work *The Evolution of Reciprocal Altruism*, which laid the ground for the biologists' interest in self-deception. Second, present-day evolutionary psychology is built on the claim that evolution has "programmed" in us certain strivings that we are unaware of.

It seems that scientists are almost swarming around the Freudian cornerstone. However, the situation is not that simple—the relation between psychoanalysis and mainstream science is polarized. On one hand, several respected researchers—neuroscientists Joseph LeDoux, Gerald Edelman, and the Nobel-laureate Eric Kandel, for example—hold that (at least some) old Freudian insights still make sense, and that the psychoanalytic way of studying man has to be taken seriously by present-day scientists. The new, promising endeavour of *neuro-psychoanalysis* also raises hopes for the integration of psychoanalysis and present-day brain research. On the other hand, Freud-bashing is almost a branch of literature: there are dozens of widely cited books the core claim of which is that Freud was a charlatan, and that psychoanalysis is fundamentally and irreparably flawed.

On this basis it is not a surprise that, although psychoanalysis and cognitive orientation have shared an interest in the unconscious for about three decades, between them there is a disagreement on even the most fundamental thing—the essence of the unconscious. When a cognitivist holds that the unconscious is just the brain, psychoanalysts have stressed that the unconscious is mental. In short, in psychoanalytic circles it is held that the mind has an unconscious part where repressed memories and desires lie, and whence they may be brought (or transformed) into the domain of consciousness.

The aim of this book is to create a conception of the "Freudian things" around the unconscious that takes seriously both the clinical data gathered in the scope of psychoanalytic clinical practice during the past 110 years, and the empirical and theoretical achievements of cognitive science and evolutionary theory. Tensions between the psychoanalytic and other views give a hint that the task is anything but easy.

When put in a larger context, those tensions appear unavoidable. First, it has to be noted that the Freudian conception of the unconscious emerged from the *zeitgeist* of nineteenth century Europe. Freud's background was in romanticism, and his studies on hypnosis, for example, were preceded by those of Mesmer. Mesmer, for his part, had to argue against a religious conception (exorcism) of hypnosis. Thus, from the perspective of the history of ideas, Freud was very far from the cognitivists that some decades later have interested themselves in consciousness and the unconscious through empirical studies, neuroscience, and metaphors taken from the information processing of computers.

Second, there is a fundamental difference between the aims of psychoanalysis and cognitive orientation. Whereas psychoanalysts are interested in psychic disorders, curing by talking, and the idiosyncratic characteristics of individuals, cognitivists focus on the general competencies of humans, and have been fascinated by the idea that thinking humans can be likened to information processing computers.

On the personal level, these differences mean that just a small number of people are genuinely interested in both psychoanalytic topics and those of a cognitive orientation. Consequently, it is difficult to find researchers who are acquainted in a profound manner with the theories and presuppositions of both those traditions. Thus, not surprisingly, the dialogue between the traditions is usually rather heated.

Given these divergences and controversies, the integrative effort of this book has to begin with the background. Thus, the first chapter is a review of which kind of phenomena researchers have tried to explain through the term "unconscious". Because the psychoanalytic view has leaned on the claim that the mind is partly unconscious, it is necessary in Chapter Two to take a look at the origins of mental terms such as "mind" and "consciousness". That way, both the "psychoanalytic" and the "cognitive" unconscious can be set in an appropriate historical context: the differences between these two conceptions will appear as reflecting certain differences between Plato and Aristotle.

The third chapter focuses on the ontological issue concerning the essence of the unconscious. As mentioned, the mental essence of the unconscious is one of the core claims of psychoanalysis. However, that idea appears extremely confusing—if a dozen psychoanalysts are asked "What does it mean that the unconscious is mental?", one is likely to get a dozen different answers. This is anything but a minor and transient deficiency of psychoanalysis: it is not possible to elaborate the psychoanalytic view in the present-day world of science, or to try to integrate it with other views, unless the ontological presuppositions concerning the unconscious are clarified.

The (interdisciplinary) fruits of taking the cognitivists' conceptualization as a starting point become clearly visible in Chapters Four and Five. In those chapters, argumentation is based on the research put forward on memory (systems), attention, implicit knowledge, neural algorithms, and the self. Psychoanalytic issues become closely connected to the several domains of present-day behavioural sciences, and they may be disputed from the viewpoint of rapidly growing scientific knowledge. That way, specific "psychoanalytic" problems become ones that are shared by other disciplines, too.

Applying the cognitivists' conceptualization leads to a reformulation of the topic of repression: repressed ideas, memories, and desires are not sought from the brain or unconscious mind any more. Instead, the crucial question is how and why certain contents do not become formed in the domain of consciousness (or, strictly speaking, in the scope of narrative self). This reformulation directs our interest to an entity that psychoanalysts since Freud have called psychic(al) apparatus, and that cognitivists refer to by the term "neural or mental machinery". Matters such as neural algorithms, "computations", and neural networks, or the brain as a system, seem to function in a "biased" manner, preventing certain ideas from emerging into consciousness. With this topic we are dealing with matters that Freud approached in his most theoretical and speculative works, namely, *Project* and his essays on metapsychology.

The reader may have got the impression that the perspectives taken above imply a radical change in the vocabulary used by clinicians—psychoanalysts should begin to learn terms used in the domains of neuroscience, non-linear dynamics and computing, and forget expressions such as "unconscious fantasy". In Chapter Six, however, it is suggested that this is not the case: scientific explanation of a phenomenon is one thing, and promoting people's well-being in psychotherapy is another. It is argued that psychoanalysts (as well as other people) have to abstract the functioning of the brain—it makes little sense to talk about one's personal matters in terms of neurophysiology. Psychoanalysts' talk about unconscious ideas should be seen as "mentalizing" the brain, i.e., talking about it *as if* it contained entities like ideas. This kind of talk is motivated and justified by the aims of therapy.

Chapter Six leans on philosopher Daniel Dennett's model of intentional, physical, and design-level explanations.

Vesa Talvitie
November 2008

CHAPTER ONE

The unconscious and the mysteries of human life

> "What, in fact, is this 'unconscious' but a high-sounding name to veil our own ignorance?"
>
> (Sully, 1878, cited in Claxton, 2005, p. 217)

I s Freud's view on the unconscious, "the cornerstone" of psychoanalysis, correct? This question, and various popular and more general alternatives ("Is Freud dead?"; "Was Freud, after all, right?"), attracts short answers, but from the scientific perspective it is misleading in at least two ways. In the first place, it is trivial, because serious scientists are seldom either completely right or completely misled, and in the second, apart from the perspective of the history of ideas, the issue of who is wrong and who is right is a minor one: the fundamental aim of science is to develop the explanations and models that best suit the phenomena under scrutiny.

Nevertheless, it is common knowledge that, in the case of psychoanalysis, it is difficult to avoid polarizations and personification: Freud was suggestive by nature and in his writings, and discussions easily slip from the factual to debate on what he really said/meant, and whether or not present-day studies support or contradict his ideas. In order not to reproduce the age-old fronts of the Freud wars, one should focus the *phenomena* that Freud and other psychoanalysts have discovered, or the *observations* and *notions* that have come to light in the context of psychoanalysis. The next step would be to create the (best possible) explanations, reflecting the current state of the art in the relevant domains of study.

One might also ask why there is so much talk about Sigmund Freud—Jung, Melanie Klein, Lacan, and the advocates of narrative psychoanalysis have joined Freud in presenting their conceptualizations of the unconscious, among other things. This book also focuses on Freud's conception, for two reasons. First, it is Freud's view that still predominates. Second, because of his background in biology and neurophysiology, the *"Freudian* unconscious" is the least difficult to comprehend from the cognitive perspective.

This book is among the growing list of studies on the relation between the psychoanalytic and the cognitive views of the unconscious (see, for example, Kandel, 1999; Kihlstrom, 1987; O'Brien & Jureidini, 2002; Pugh, 2002; Searle, 1992, 151–173), and the "psychoanalytic" and the "cognitive" unconscious in particular are under discussion here. The origins of the psychoanalytic unconscious are clear (Freud's writings at the end of the nineteenth century), and Kihlstrom, Barnhardt, and Tataryn (1992, p. 788) traced the concept of the "cognitive unconscious" to Paul Rozin and the year 1976. However, Jean Piaget had already studied the relation between the "affective" (psychoanalytic) and the "cognitive" unconscious in his 1973 article.

According to Kihlstrom, Barnhardt, and Tataryn,

> . . . the psychological unconscious documented by latter-day scientific psychology is quite different from what Sigmund Freud and his psychoanalytic colleagues had in mind in fin de siècle Vienna. Their unconscious was hot and wet; it seethed with lust and anger; it was hallucinatory, primitive, and irrational. The unconscious of contemporary psychology is kinder and gentler than that and more reality bound and rational, even if it is not entirely cold and dry. In any event, the evidence for the [cognitive] unconscious discussed by Greenwald (1992) *in no way provides evidence for psychodynamic ideas.* [1992, p. 789; my emphasis]

Generally speaking, researchers on both sides agree with Kihlstrom, Barnhardt, and Tataryn's characterization in terms of the dichtomy hot and wet–cold and dry (for example, Power & Brewin, 1991; Woody & Phillips, 1995). However, the last sentence of the citation is extremely controversial: the question concerning evidence in favor of the psychoanalytic concept is often given rapid and short answers on both sides.

Part of the confusions around the two types of unconscious arise from the fact that the concept has been used to explain many different kinds of phenomena. In order to clarify the discussion about the psychoanalytic and the cognitive unconscious, the phenomena behind the unconscious(es) is approached below in terms of two categories.

First, there are those that somehow astonish and/or frighten us, or at least are difficult to explain in a reasonable manner—they are *oddities* of human experience and behaviour. Second, humans possess *competencies* that are not based on conscious processing— we are able to drive a car without thinking of the pedals the whole time, and can produce correct sentences without having the rules of grammar in the domain of our consciousness, for example. These two traditions behind the term "unconscious" did not suddenly pop up, either when Freud began to create his theories at the turn of the nineteenth and and twentieth centuries, or when cognitivists became interested in the unconscious in the last few decades of the twentieth century.

Before turning to study those oddities and competencies in a more detailed manner, I would like to introduce briefly two ideas presented by Guy Claxton, the author of *The Wayward Mind: An Intimate History of the Unconscious* (2004). First, he suggests that people's explanations for those oddities have changed over time from the "outward" to the "inward" stories (*ibid.*, 1–26). The ancient Greeks, for example, explained them in terms of external forces and agents (gods), whereas present-day people use terminology that refers to man's internal processes and biological entities (repressed memories and neurotransmitters, for example).

Claxton (*ibid.*, pp. 155–189) also holds that explanations of these oddities fall into three categories: the supernatural, the physiological, and the psychological. *Supernatural explanations* refer to different kinds of gods, spirits, and (external) forces. Explanations of present-day neuroscience (and, for the most part, psychiatry) refer-ring to entities such as neurotransmitters and neural networks are *physiological*; the Ancient Greeks' ideas about bodily "humours" could be seen as an early predecessor of this type of explanation. Current "folk psychology", or people's common-sense views on the determination of human behaviour, is a good example of a pure *psychological explanation*; no stand is taken on how entities such as psychic complexes and unconscious fears might be described in terms of neuroscience.

Supernatural outward explanations have not vanished. In the domain of alternative medicine, for example, reference is often made to different kinds of energies, the existence of which has not—at least yet—been verified scientifically. In another case, a north-European protestant vicar and Master of Theology was accused in 2005 of assaulting his wife, but claimed that her injuries were caused by evil forces, and that she should be treated by an exorcist.

The unconscious and oddities of human experience and behaviour

Edwards and Jacobs (2003, pp. 2–27) and Claxton (2004) mention numerous phenomena that have been explained by referring to the man's unconscious. Some of these (and some others) are described below under three headings: bodily and motor reactions, altered states of consciousness, and stream of consciousness.

Bodily and motor reactions

Compulsive behaviour, epileptic seizure, ADHD, Tourette's syn-drome, psychosomatic disorder, and panic disorder are contempo-rary names or "labels" for certain oddities of human behaviour. When people lacked contemporary psychological concepts and knowledge about neurophysiology, and they believed their worlds to be inhabited by gods and mysterious forces, it was reasonable to present supernatural explanations for this kind of phenomenon. As trust in rational reasoning and scientific study slowly began to gain ground during the Enlightenment, people also began to turn to psychological and physiological "inward" explanations.

The term "the unconscious" appeared in Western languages less than three hundred years ago (see Chapter Two). At the beginning of the 1800s it was not possible to explain these oddities fully in those terms, although it did help in making sense of certain puzzling aspects of human life.

Currently, there seems to be a battle going on over the best explanation for these phenomena. Freud built his psychological explanations of psychiatric disorders around the concept of the "unconscious", and present-day psychotherapists of different orientations still lean on psychological explanations. On the other hand, contemporary "biological" psychiatry has produced physical explanations—in terms of neurotransmitters and dysfunctions in certain neurobiological systems, for instance. On the level of theory (or the philosophy of science), the relation between psychological and (neuro)physiological explanations is rather a tricky issue, and it is studied in detail in Chapter Six. Anyway, in practice, doctors (and researchers) often recommend patients to take drugs *and* to go into psychotherapy.

Altered states of consciousness

When we are sleeping and dreaming we do not have conscious perceptions about what surrounds us, but we should, nevertheless, consider dreaming to be a conscious state. What are we conscious of while we are dreaming? The world of dreams closely resembles the perceptions and ideas we form when we are awake, but dreams also contain weird elements. They seem to tell us something about something, but what, and about what? Not surprisingly, religions have leaned on supernatural matters when addressing this question. Many researchers, Freud being the best-known of them, have developed psychological explanations: dreams tell us something about the unconscious mind. Nowadays we also have the physical explanations offered by neuroscientists.

Most of us have read about states of trance, mysterious religious experiences, and automatic writing. Such phenomena have been conceptualized in many ways in the domain of psychiatry. Someone diagnosed as having multiple personality disorder (MPD; currently known as dissociative identity disorder, DID), seems to have several—possibly even as many as a dozen—different personalities.

Each of these may have a separate identity, and behaviour may change radically in the transition from one personality state to another. When the person concerned is in one personality state, he or she is often unaware of the existence of the other personalities. The implication seems to be that there may be in man desires, attitudes, and habits that are hidden except in certain states of personality.

It is relatively easy to sketch different kinds of supernatural and psychological explanations for MPD, but it is more difficult to imagine what a pure physiological explanation might consist of.

Stream of consciousness

We can often manage our stream of consciousness. For example, if we find ourselves in a shop and wonder what we came for, we might succeed in bringing the reason to mind by reasoning that we were going to make a cake, and we had no baking soda at home. At other times, however, we cannot remember even the most obvious things, or our memories show themselves to be distorted. On the other hand, unwelcome ideas that we try *not to* think about often flash up into our consciousness. Ideas come and go, often without being summoned, and the same holds with moods: the phenomenon called "affective disorder(s)" in present-day psychiatry causes a lot of suffering.

Obsessions and compulsions, mood disorders, and, indeed, also creativity, could easily be seen as mysteries that are open to various explanations. Anyone suffering from obsessive ideas or a low mood may feel that an external agent or force is persecuting or controlling her/him—and this is as true today as it has been for centuries. Similarly, when somebody possesses exceptional mental abilities—typical of shamans (in the past) and of outstanding scientists or artists today—her/his "genius" is often explained in terms of the supernatural or the mysterious.

It is tempting to think that beneath the surface of consciousness lies some kind of machinery or set of rules that determines the nature of our conscious states and of which we are unaware. Thus, Freud's notion of the *psychic apparatus* was one of his recurring themes, and the domain of cognitive science has its *neural machinery* and *neural algorithms*.

*   *   *

There are still other phenomena that appear to refer to the unconscious but do not fall into any of the categories mentioned above. One of these is self-deception—a person's ability to deceive him/herself into believing something that he or she knows not to be true—which has attracted the interest of thinkers from Aristotle and St Augustine to Jean-Paul Sartre and present-day scholars. The conscious–unconscious dichotomy is also used to refer to cultural presuppositions, which direct everyone's thinking and construction of reality (see, for example, Hodgkiss, 2001). Thus, sexist or racist attitudes might prevail in a culture, for example, but may remain hidden from its members.

It was the oddities that gave rise to the psychonalytic view of the unconscious: hypnosis, patients' hysterical (Anna O, Dora) and phobic (little Hans) reactions, as well as dreams, awoke Freud's interest. He explained those oddities through the following logic. What lies behind them are repressed instinctual impulses, wishes, memories, and fears, which remain beyond consciousness through the agency of censorship. However, these contents possess a drive to reach consciousness, and censorship cannot control that drive completely. This repression is what gives rise to psychic disorders, dreams, and different kinds of slips, all of which represent the repressed content in a symbolic form.

Freud formulated a neurophysiological basis for psychology in his *Project for a Scientific Psychology* (1895). However, that project remained unfinished and was published only after his death. He still had hopes of anchoring his theories in neurophysiology, but they were never realized and the Freudian explanation of the oddities is thus psychological. Present-day neuropsychoanalysis has revived interest in explaining these "oddities" neurophysiologically.

Competencies: cognitive orientation and the unconscious

It could be said that psychoanalysis has explored the "dark" side of the unconscious—odd and frightening matters and psychological causes of suffering. The coin has another side, too: researchers in cognitive orientation have been astonished at the human ability to perform complicated tasks without conscious control. A lay-person thinks nothing of the fact that one can ride a bicycle or drive a car while thinking of very different things (upon reaching one's destination one does not necessarily remember anything about the trip). A cognitivist researcher, however, realizes that riding a bicycle is a very complex task: one has to take into account many things concerning both the surroundings and one's bodily movements. When we are able to perform such tasks without thinking consciously about it, we might legitimately attribute it to the unconscious.

Take birds, for example, which are able to fly the same route annually from, say, Ireland to Pihtiputaa. There is reason to suppose that this competence is not based on conscious reasoning (". . . and this seems to be Copenhagen . . ."), which again implies that conscious processing is not a precondition for intelligent behaviour in biological organisms. The computer science branch of cognitive science approaches these matters by building computer simulations (chess computers among them) of human competencies, which are assumed to give hints about what kind of systems in the brain might produce actions performed without conscious control.

Before moving on to the empirical research on unconscious competencies, I should mention that altered states of consciousness, as well as unpredictability in the stream of consciousness, also has another side. Peak, or "flow", experience, as popularized by Mihalyi Csikszentmihalyi (1990), is an example of the "positive" altered state of consciousness. It refers to when someone is able to use her/his capabilities more efficiently than normal, and Bob Beamon's world record (890 cm) in the long jump in the Mexico Olympics of 1968 (the previous world record was 835 cm) is often used as an example.

While obsessive disorder is at the dark end of the stream-of-consciousness continuum, at the other end is creativity and sudden insights. Researchers often tell stories about how the solution to a difficult scientific problem just popped into their mind while they were thinking of completely different matters. This "Eureka effect" (see Perkins, 2000) is familiar to those who engage in remodelling and design.

Now let us go to the laboratory. Competencies based on unconscious cognitive processes have been studied extensively within several research paradigms, and there is a multitude of concepts describing them: semantic priming, tacit knowledge, implicit knowledge, procedural knowledge, implicit learning, implicit memory, subliminal perpection, non-declarative memory (for references, see Talvitie & Ihanus, 2002, pp. 1311–1312). Henceforth, the term "implicit knowledge" is used to refer to all these paradigms; that is, to experience, thought, and action that is affected by past events, which the person concerned cannot consciously remember (Kihlstrom, Shames, & Dorfman, 1996, p. 3).

It was in the 1980s that cognitive scientists became increasingly interested in consciousness, and thus non-conscious skills and competencies also came to the fore in empirical research. The core idea of implicit knowledge has been in the air for a much longer time, however (see, for example, Ryle, 1949, pp. 28–32). In the realm of implicit memory, the conceptual ground was laid by Ebbinghaus, who had a broader view of memory than his contemporaries: he saw it not only as conscious collection, but also in terms of "test-performance influences". Both historically and currently, the study of implicit knowledge has incorporated empirical research and clinical notions concerning the competences of brain-injury patients. At the end of the nineteenth century, Sergei Korsakoff found that, although amnesiacs did not remember having had an electric shock, they knew what he was going to do with the shock apparatus (because, after all, they remembered something about having been given the shock) (Masson & Graf, 1993, p. 2).

John MacCurdy is known to have found evidence of implicit knowledge in 1928 (de Gelder, de Haan, & Heywood, 2001, p. ix). He met a patient with Korsakoff syndrome, typically having severe problems with his short-term memory. He was told MacCurdy's name and address, which he promptly forgot. However, when he was given ten options of forenames, surnames, and street names and numbers, he chose the right ones. This is evidence of one property of implicit knowledge: it often shows in so-called forced-choice guessing.

The origins of the term implicit learning can be determined more exactly: Arthur Reber introduced it in 1967. Reber studied artificial grammar learning, and his experiments followed a particular logic. In the first phase his subjects were presented with series of letter strings (BBAAB and GGJJG, for example), which they were asked to memorize. In the second phase they were told that letter strings indeed had a grammar. They were presented with still more letter strings and were asked to state which of them were grammatically appropriate (like those in phase one). Although they could not say what the grammar was, they were able to tell which series possessed it. The core issue here is that the research on implicit learning seems to indicate that the unconscious is able to deal with abstractions such as grammar (Berry 1997).

The term "subliminal perception" also originates from the end of the nineteenth century, but it was not until the 1970s that the phenomenon became an object of intensive study. It is rooted in a tradition of research in which the focus is on how stimuli, usually words, that are flashed subliminally affect the processing of following stimuli (another word). It has been found that, although subjects do not recognize subliminally presented "doctor", they might recognize the following "nurse" more quickly. Subliminally presented stimuli are thought to activate semantic networks. The notion of subliminal stimuli is familiar to many because of the debate surrounding subliminal marketing (Merikle, 2000).

For a non-specialist, the differences between implicit memory, implicit learning, and subliminal perception are of minor importance—it seems only to be a question of the methods through which the competencies of the unconscious are studied. Empirical studies on unconscious competencies involve several stages, and the reports are often full of technical details. This easily obscures the logic behind the experiments. Most of studies follow the same logic, however, which is explained below. One classic study is then described by way of illustration.

First, subjects are presented with a stimulus, or they perform a task. The second phase is conducted to show that they did not (consciously) perceive the stimulus, or that they did not notice or remember a certain aspect of the task. In the third phase they perform a task in which the stimuli presented in the first phase are of help. If the presenting of the stimuli in the first phase (of which the subjects remained unconscious) improves the performance in the third phase, it is an indication that unconscious memory/learning/knowledge affected performance.

In the first phase of Kunst-Wilson and Zajonc's (1980) beautiful classic experiment, the subjects were presented with different kinds of irregular octagons. Octagons are difficult to remember, and, not surprisingly, in the second phase recognition of those presented in the first was very poor. The subjects were then presented with new octagons and with those from the first phase, and they were asked to say which ones they liked best. Although they could not say which octagons they had seen in phase one, these were the ones they liked more. Thus, the fact that they had seen them in phase one affected their performance in the third phase, even though they did not recognize them or remember having seen them.

Outside laboratories, clinical observations of brain injuries having caused blindsight, prosopagnosia (the inability to recognize faces), and different kinds of amnesia favour the idea of implicit knowledge. For example, although a patient with prosopagnosia does not recognize faces, his or her skin conductance may be different with familiar faces—the recognizion is unconscious (Shimamura, 1993; Young, 1994).

It should also be noted that within all branches of the study of implicit knowledge there has been debate on whether the phenomena found in laboratories are real, and on the technical details of the experiments: the classic articles and critiques include those by Holender (1986) and Shanks & St John (1994). The main criticism is that the subjects were indeed conscious of the stimuli presented in phase one, but were—for several reasons—not able to retrieve them later. This is of minor importance in the context of this work—what is unchallenged is that people are often not aware of previous events that affect current behaviour. Empirical findings have also shown a connection to the brain: behind implicit knowledge on the one hand and explicit knowledge on the other have been found distinct neural systems (see, for example, Squire & Kandel, 1999, pp. 23–67).

Thus, it is clear that, although not later (consciously) remembered, events (or "stimuli") may give rise to preferences (one likes or fears something because of the previous event) and behavioural dispositions (certain behaviour is triggered).

*   *   *

These kinds of matters have been revealed in laboratories following stimuli such as word flashes, strings of letters, and octagons. It makes no sense to think that implicit knowledge is restricted to the laboratory, however; it appears in issues related to psychoanalysis, too. Thus, we might suppose that the voice of the primary care-taker has been coded by the implicit knowledge system, that panic attacks are triggred by stimuli that activate certain neural represen-tations of the implicit knowledge system, and that implicit know-ledge is responsible for "free" associations and transference reactions, for example. Erdelyi (1996, p. 182) put forward the notion that phenomena revealed in research on implicit knowledge could be seen as "laboratory homologues" to clinically significant matters such as maladaptive behaviour and hysterical symptoms. Freud held that patients suffered from "reminiscences", and Erdelyi put that in terms of cognitive science: past events appear in procedural forms but not in the declarative memory.

The integration of the psychoanalytic and cognitive views of the unconscious

Researchers are not usually interested in the unconscious as such—they have, rather, found a certain phenomenon, and the term "unconscious" (or "tacit/implicit knowledge") is part of their effort to explain it. Thus, behind the term "unconscious" are a number of phenomena referred to above as oddities and competencies. Inter-est in the former prevails in the domains of psychiatry and clinical psychology, while the latter falls within the realm of empirical lab-oratory research (the study of brain damage putting a clinical slant on implicit knowledge, however). The claim that it is possible to explain both different kinds of oddities and several competencies through one conception of the unconscious gives rise to scepti-cism: one could state that behind several and different phenomena there are probably also several and different psychological mecha-nisms and neural structures. According to this kind of thinking, the term "unconscious" merely creates the illusion of a shared inter-est among proponents of psychoanalysis and of the cognitive orientation.

However, both psychoanalysis and cognitive neuroscience wholeheartedly accept the claim that our activities are determined for the most part by matters of which we are unaware. It sounds rather unlikely that there might be two classes of matters of which we are not aware—one for psychoanalysis, one for cognitive neuroscience. Thus, it is reasonable to search for a common ground for the psychoanalytic and cogntive views.

With the Freudian unconscious there is a notable and fundamental problem: nobody has ever identified what kind of entity the unconscious is supposed to be. In his earlier psychoanalytic writings, Freud boldly emphasized that the unconscious is mental: In "The unconscious" he stated that ". . . the conventional equation of the psychical with the conscious is totally inexpedient" (Freud, 1915e, pp. 167–168). In *Introductory Lectures on Psycho-Analysis* (1916–1917), he held that "The first of these unpopular assertions made by psychoanalysis declares that mental processes are in themselves unconscious and that of all mental life it is only certain individual acts and portions that are conscious" (*ibid.*, p. 21). On the next page he is quite solemn: ". . . yet I can assure you that the hypothesis of there being unconscious mental processes paves the way to a decisive new orientation in the world and in science" (*ibid.*, p. 22) In *The Ego and the Id* we find the following statement:

> The division of the psychical into what is conscious and what is unconscious is the fundamental premise of psycho-analysis; and it alone makes it possible for psycho-analysis to understand the pathological processes in mental life . . . and to find a place for them in the framework of science." [Freud, 1923b, p. 13]

However, in *An Outline of Psycho-Analysis*, one of his last works, the tone had become more cautious:

> We know two kinds of things about what we call our psyche (or mental life): firstly, its bodily organ and scene of action, the brain (or nervous system) and, on the other hand, our acts of consciousness . . . Everything that lies between is unknown to us, and the data do not include any direct relation between these two terminal points of our knowledge. If it existed, it would at the most afford an exact localization of the processes of consciousness and would give us no help towards understanding them. [Freud, 1940a, pp. 145–146]

Thus, from this citation, it is understandable that Freud's followers might have felt confused or even suspicious about the existence and essence of the unconscious. However, these words are not at all indicative of post-Freudian psychoanalysis. Quite the contrary: the mental unconscious has been, and still is, the cornerstone of Freud's legacy. It is difficult to find a psychoanalytic text from the past six decades that challenges the idea that the unconscious is mental. It is equally difficult to find a text that explains what the term "mental" means when placed in front of "unconscious". The vagueness of the concept "mental unconscious" indicates that the Freudian view needs demystification—i.e., more focused discussion on what it is and is not.

In psychoanalytic writings, the unconscious is also often described in a rather poetic tone. Things often happen in psychoanalysis and other psychotherapies that astonish both participants, and they might be experienced as mysterious. The concept unconscious aims at *explaining mysteries*, and it is weird when *it* is called a mystery. From the perspective of the history of science, mysteries have been resolved through discoveries such as magnetism and electricity. Thus, if there is mysteriousness surrounding the unconscious, it means only that our knowledge is impartial, and we should go more deeply into it.

Thus, cognitivists and psychoanalysts disagree on the essence of the unconscious: the former consider it "a neural thing", and the latter see it is a "mental" one—they presume that the mind contains an unconscious part. It seems obvious that we can proceed with the integration of psychoanalytic and cognitive views only after having faced questions such as: what does the term "mental" refer to; what is the mind; is it possible that part of it is unconscious? Behind these straightforward questions there are several more fundamental and complicated issues that could be formulated as follows.

- The term "unconscious" is logically dependent on the term consciousness. There are several terms in English with mental connotations (mind, psyche, consciousness), and each of them has several meanings and origins in many languages.
- We cannot make sense of the Freudian idea that the unconscious is of the mind before we have an agreed idea of what the mind is.
- Freud wrote in German, and used both *Seele* and *Psyche* when stressing the mental essence of the unconscious.
- The biological basis of the mind and of consciousness is still a mystery in the context of both science and philosophy. This fact is probably also reflected in the study of the unconscious.

- Could the "Freudian" unconscious be studied by using equipment developed for present-day neuroscience, and if not, why not?
- Could mechanical apparatus (computers, robots) possess a mind? Whether they could or not, could the processess and structures of the unconscious be seen in terms of information processing and neural algorithms?
- Could there be two types of unconscious, the "psychoanalytic" and the "cognitive"? Alternatively, do psychoanalysis and the cognitive orientation study the same unconscious using different methods and from different perspectives (whatever that may mean)?

What follows, therefore, is a study of the origins of mental concepts from the perspective of the history of ideas. The later chapters do not logically depend on Chapter Two, and thus a reader lacking enthusiasm for the history of ideas may skip it. However, the following chapter enables one to make sense of the reasons that lie behind the tension between psychoanalysis and cognitive orientation and the Freud wars. For example, it demonstrates that we can find two traditions behind the term "unconscious". The first of these—which leads to present-day notions of the cognitive unconscious—begins from Aristotle's works on logic.

The second line of thought, represented currently by proponents of psychoanalysis, is along the lines of unconscious agencies and sophisticated unconscious states ("dipsychism"). It originates in Plato's ideas, and the spirit of romanticism is also evident in Freud's thinking.

CHAPTER TWO

Historical context of the tension between the cognitive and the psychoanalytic unconscious

W hen trying to reach what Freud meant by claiming that the unconscious is *mental*, and that the *mind* contains an unconscious part, the contents of which might be prevented from being brought into the domain of *consciousness*, the first task is to study the references of those mental terms. However, it has to be remembered that Freud wrote in German, and thus never used those terms—he talked about *Bewusstheit*, *Psyche*, and *Seele*, and the latter terms have both been translated into English as *mind*.

The layman's intuition concerning words (concepts) and their translation from one language to another goes something like this: in the world there are definable matters, and each language contains names for these matters; ideas presented in language A can be translated into language B by simply searching for the corresponding words. This intuition is misleading, however. The best known attack against it was made by Ludwig Wittgenstein in his works after *Tractatus Logico-philosophicus* (especially Wittgenstein, 1953).

Thus, Paul Macdonald opens his book *History of The Concept of Mind: Speculations about Soul, Mind and Spirit from Homer to Hume* in a pessimistic tone:

The history of the concepts of mind and soul is a complex and twisted network of many paths, each path strewn with obstacles, dead ends, false and hidden beginnings, relapses into old ways of thinking and forward leaps of imaginative projection. One of the principal problems is to sort out exactly which issue is being addressed when one holds up for scrutiny any one of the numerous terms involved in the ancestry of the modern concept of mind or soul . . . In other words, if there is no consensus on what the concept of *mind* picks out or what it makes reference to, if the historian cannot appeal to a readily identifiable conceptual item, then how can any effort to trace its ancestry ever be confident that discussions of an earlier version are indeed versions of the same thing? [Macdonald, 2003, p. 1]

Thus, the most fundamental obstacle encountered in the study of the mind and the mental is that there is no consensus on what the words mean and to which entities they refer. The conflict between the psychoanalytic and cognitive views concerning the unconscious has surely something to do with this fundamental problem, and so it is appropriate to take a look at the historical background of mental terms.

The origins of some mental terms

The English words mind, consciousness, soul, and spirit

The terms "consciousness", "mind", and "psyche" are often used interchangeably: we can say either that an idea came to mind, or that it came into consciousness. It also usually makes no difference if we talk about mental or psychic processes. However, these English words have different roots.

Chambers Encyclopedic English Dictionary defines the term consciousness as follows: "1 the state of being conscious. 2 awareness. 3 Psychol. The physical and mental state of being awake and fully aware of one's environment, thoughts and feelings".

"Conscious" comes from the Latin words *con* (together) and *sci* (knowing). Thus, it originally meant that two persons know the same fact. According to *The Oxford English Dictionary*, the word in that meaning is known to have appeared in 1651. In the sense in which we use it (i.e., the definition given in *Chambers Dictionary*), it appeared for the first time almost a hundred years later, in 1746—only about a century before Sigmund Freud's birth. Thus, our forebears had quite different ideas concerning the nature of man. It is also important to note that the term *conscience* has the same root as consciousness. This means that the word "consciousness" connotes with Judeo-Christian ideas concerning guilt (Ryle, 1949, p. 24).

The Oxford English Dictionary defines "mind" (from the Latin root *mens*) as "The seat of a person's consciousness, thoughts, volitions, and feelings ...". In its current sense, the term is four hundred years older than the word "consciousness" (1340). The authors of the dictionary regret that "Unfortunately the word mind has been almost universally employed to signify both that which thinks, and the phenomena of thinking" (hence *mental*, the adjective form of the word, is often needed).

The meanings of the English words *soul* (888) and *spirit* (1250) sometimes come quite near to that of the "mind". The important difference between the "mind" on the one hand, and the "soul" and "spirit" on the other is the following: "the mind" does not (necessarily) contain any religious presuppositions, whereas "soul" and "spirit" are closely related to the Christian religion and to theology. Spirit also refers to a liquid that is supposed to give life to humans.

"Psyche" in the pre-Socratic period of Greek, and in the Old Testament

The term *psyche* (psychic, psychology) has remarkably longer roots than "consciousness" and "mind". "Psyche" comes from a Greek word, transliterated as psyche. It was used in Homeric poems (*ca.* 750 BC), the earliest extant literature. In English, psyche is translated as both "mind" and "soul". In the minds of present-day Western people, the term is the other half of the dichotomy between the mind and the body. Originally, especially in pre-Socratic thought, the picture was completely different. Homeric poems contain several words related to the term "mind": *ker* (life-force), *noos* (intellectual activity), *aion* (vital force), *thymos* (source of emotions), *menos* (an impulse toward a specific action), for example. The original meaning of the word psyche was "life", but it has several meanings in Homeric poetry. In certain places the best translation would be "the life principle", and in others it comes close to the English words the "self" and "person": it refers to constant features of a certain person. Those features were not necessarily always "mental"—Homer sometimes referred to constant features of the outward appearance, for example (Gundert, 2000; Macdonald, 2003, pp. 2–22; Wright & Potter, 2000)

In pre-Socratic thinking on the subject of (what we would call) the mind also had a clinical aspect. Hippocrates (or several Hippocratic writers between *ca.* 450–350 BC) included in medicine issues that from the present-day perspective would fall in the domain of psychiatry—some of the clinical practices in Ancient Greece resemble twentieth-century psychodynamic therapy (Ellenberger, 1970, pp. 40–43).

Descartes talked about *animal spirits* in the seventeenth century, and in the nineteenth century Mesmer explained his findings in terms of *animal magnetism.* These terms make sense only if we realize that the Greek word *pneuma* was translated into Latin as *spiritus* (breath), and *anima* is the Latin equivalent of *psyche* (Macdonald, 2003, p. 2).

Present-day Western thinking is rooted in the Ancient Greek, and also the Judeo-Christian tradition. The Old Testament alone contains a host of words that are translated as mind or soul in English: *nepesh* (the most primitive meaning is "throat or gullet", then "desire or longing", "life or vital force", and finally, "me or I"); *ruach* (see the next paragraph); *leb* ("heart", "will or intention", "conscious or conscience", "me or I") (Macdonald, 2003, pp. 2–3). It is worth noting that the idea of the soul as a distinct entity from the body is alien to the Old Testament (*ibid.*, p. 90)—it is characteristic only of the writings of the New Testament.

In the previous chapter I mentioned Claxton's (2004) claim that in the history of mankind, people's explanations of mysterious phenomena have moved from "outward" stories to "inward" stories (pp. 1–26). From that perspective it is easy to accept Macdonald's (2003, p. 3) general model concerning the process of how words referring to "mental" matters have evolved in different languages. At first, the word means something concrete, which is outside of man (wind, for example). Gradually, the meaning changes, and it begins to refer to something concrete that is inside man—the heart, for example. Following the next shift, the word refers to an abstract property of man—life force, for example, and finally the word is reflexive (I, me, self). According to Macdonald (*ibid*.), in the case of the Hebrew word *ruach*, the process was the following: (1) wind; (2) breath or the organ of breathing; (3) one who breathes, an individual; and (4) me or I.

* * *

Given the Latin (mind, consciousness) and Greek (psyche) origins of mental terms, we can draw the following general conclusions: the terms "mental" and "mind" are based on the distinction between *mind and matter*, whereas the term "psyche" focuses on the difference between *living and non-living organisms*. The former (Latin) perspective could be called philosophical, and the latter (Greek) biological. As will be shown later, an additional perspective emerged in the seventeenth century: certain aspects of human essence became accessible in mechanical terms. The building of the first computers four centuries later brought mechanical vocabulary ("information processing", for example) to the core of the cognitive orientation.

Based on the considerations above, the following question arises: when psychoanalysts emphasize that the unconscious is mental, does it mean that it (1) consists of "mental stuff"; (2) that it is a biological (living, organic, neurophysiological) entity; or that (3) it cannot be described in mechanical terms?

The first option would make Freud's claim concerning the essence of the unconscious a philosophical issue. However, Freud himself would not like that, since he had a strong antipathy towards philosophy. Probably he would be more comfortable with the second option, because it would fit well with his background in neuroscience (as well as with the current views of cognitivists). The third option contradicts both Freud's (hydraulic methaphors in metapsychology) and cognitive scientists' (computer metaphor) ease with mechanical vocabulary.

Mental terms may refer to various human aspects or competencies: intelligence, life-force, emotions, free will, conscience, learning, motivation, goal-directed behaviour, memory, the qualitative aspect of consciousness (the ability to feel emotions), and imagery. To which of these aspects would the word "mental", placed in front of "unconscious", refer?

It seems that the answer is almost all of them: we can clearly discount just the qualitative aspect of consciousness, because Freud (1915e) held that we should talk about unconscious emotions only in a metaphorical sense. Talk about repressed memories and wishes implies that the unconscious concerns *memory* and *motivation*, and the idea that it could express itself in a symbolic form (in dreams, disorders, and slips) presupposes that it is able to process matters in an *intelligent* manner. The ability of the unconscious to learn and react to changing conditions implies *flexibility*. In claiming it embodies fantasies, psychoanalysts even connect the unconscious to the human capability to create and manipulate mental images in the domain of consciousness.

Plato and Aristotle: the forerunners of psychoanalysis and the cognitive orientation

Psychoanalysis and the cognitive orientation do not just happen to represent differing perspectives on the unconscious; they represent also differing interests and influences of different aspects of Western thinking. Dreyfus (1972) and Gardner (1985) are respected for their critical introductions to the origins of the cognitive orientation, and Ellenberger (1970), Sulloway (1979) and Kitcher (1992) could be seen as their counterparts in the domain of psychoanalysis. Comparison of psychoanalysis and the cognitive orientation reveals certain general differences that are similar to those between Plato and Aristotle: what is common to Plato and psychoanalysis is motivation and certain "mentalism", and to cognitivists and Aristotle are reason and intellect. In terms of the mind/brain, the former focus on agencies and dynamics, and the latter on processes.

Plato

Robinson (2000, p. 39) states that Plato's (427–347 BC) works were "the first fully articulated account of the relationship between soul (*psyche*) and body (*soma*) in Western literature". According to Macdonald (2003, p. 42), the Socratic (or early Platonic) view of the nature of the human being "is clearly some sort of dualism, but what sort of dualism is not yet decided; whether the soul is mortal or immortal, material or immaterial, is left in the air".

In his early works Plato credited Socrates with advocating that the psyche had a dominant role over the body: it was the cognitive and moral agent, and it reflected the true nature of a person. Bodily desires (towards food, drink, and sex, for example) were different from the desires of the psyche (knowledge and goodness). *Charmenides* contains an analogy that illustrates Plato's early view on the relation between psyche and body: according to Socrates, the psyche is to the body as the head is to the eyes. This implies that the psyche is superior to the body, and that the body has functions only in terms of the psyche (Macdonald, 2003, pp. 37–46; Robinson, 2000, pp. 39–45)

The psyche of Plato's early writings consisted of two parts (or aspects): reason and non-rational ("gut") impulses. Different kinds of bipartite models were common in Ancient Greece, but Plato's later tripartite model was first of its kind. It posited that the psyche comprised (1) reason (*logos*, located in the head); (2) spirit (*thumos*, chest); and (3) desire or appetite (*epithumos*, stomach). Each of these parts or aspects had its own desires, pleasures, and pains of its own: reason loves wisdom, truth, and learning; the spirit aspires to honour and victory; objects of desire include money and profit. Plato illustrated his view of aspects of the psyche through a well-known comparison with the chariot, which consisted of the *driver* (reason), *a noble, white horse* (higher emotions, spirit), and *a black, base horse* (desire, appetite) (Claxton, 2005, pp. 79–85; Macdonald, 2003, 46–54; Robinson 2000, pp. 44–55).

The ancient Greeks first conceptualized problems of human life as "outward stories" in terms of natural forces, and after that as conflicts between gods. By the seventh century BC the gods began to lose their influence, and "inward stories" gained ground—initially in terms of connecting emotions and behavioral tendencies to bodily organs. Plato's bipartite model portrayed human life as a battle between the psyche and the body. From today's perspective, the shift to the tripartite model had important consequences: it set conflicts *inside the psyche* in the form of tensions between the three inner agents.

There is a certain similarity between Plato's doctrine of tripartition and the psychoanalytic perspective. Both emphasize the *dynamics* of the mind and intrapsychic conflicts, although Plato considered those dynamics conscious: the driver and the horses were

transparent to each other (Claxton, 2005, p. 81). Freud was not igno-
rant of Plato's works, and the resemblance between the tripartite
model and Freud's structural model is evident: driver = reason–
ego, white horse = spirit–superego, black horse = desire–id (Tallis,
2002, p. 62; Claxton, 2005, p. 179). Claxton (2005, p. 179) explicates—
tongue in cheek—Freud's anthropomorphosization of the mind by
suggesting that the Freudian internal agents were a rather nervous
bank clerk, a Puritan priest, and a sex-crazed monkey. Perhaps the
most anthropomorphic of Freud's psychic instances was "censorship", however, the task of which is to "decide" which ideas are
allowed to enter consciousness.

Aristotle

Throughout Aristotle's (384–322 BC) work runs a line of thought
that differs significantly from Plato's (substance) dualism. Aristotle
was interested in matters that fell within (our) concept of the
natural sciences, and his view is often characterized as biological—
he considered man to be a rational animal. Not surprisingly, for
Christian theology, Aristotle's biologism has always been a problem—Plato's mentalism has been easier to fuse to it (see Lindberg,
1992). In general, Aristotle's central aim was to anchor the psyche
in the activities of the body.

He presented many analogies in order to communicate his idea
on the nature of the mind. He considered the body and the mind to
be like matter and form, subject and predicate, or eyes and sight
(van der Eijk, 2000; Macdonald, 2003, pp. 54–71). His thinking could
even be claimed to represent property dualism. This is a view that
is widely advocated in present-day science, suggesting that the
mind is a property of the physiological processes of the brain and
the body (this will later be called the "two-sphere view"). However,
Aristotle also assumed that there was a part of the psyche that was
distinct from the body and was immortal: intellect (*nous*), or the
capacity for insight and reflection (Macdonald, 2003, pp. 65–66; van
der Eijk, 2000, p. 70).

Aristotle's works cover some topics, such as acrasia (weakness
of will), forgetting, and dreams, which are also the focus of psychoanalysis, although his work was more significant for cognitivists.
According to van der Eijk (2000, p. 57), Aristotle's remarks on the

domain of the mind and its relation to the body ". . . perhaps more than those of any other ancient philosopher, continue to be welcomed as stimulating contributions to contemporary debate in the philosophy of mind and the cognitive sciences" (see also Wedin, 1988, pp. 18–22). From a more general perspective, Aristotle's most significant contributions are in the domain of logic: he is often called the "father of logic".

A researcher in the humanities may well ask what on earth logic has to do with psychology and the unconscious. He/she may also have wondered why so many great names in the history of (cognitive) psychology—Aristotle, Leibniz, Descartes, Alan Turing, Marvin Minsky, John von Neumann, to mention just a few—were logicians or mathematicians. A very brief answer might be as follows: logic and mathematics are efforts to *present human thinking in a formal way*. This makes cognitivists' fascination with computers comprehensible: computers are able to make mathematical analysis tick—in playing chess, for example.

In creating his foundations of logic, Aristotle aimed at explicating the rules of human thinking—why and how the sentences "Socrates is a man" and "Men are mortal" lead to the sentence "Socrates is mortal", for example. If the first two (so-called presuppositions) are true, and if they are manipulated accurately in one's mind, one reaches a conclusion that is also true. Aristotle created a language of symbols for logic, which enabled him to present presuppositions and conclusions in an abstract form. We could say that he re-symbolized the thought process.

How do we know which sentences are worth putting together in order to arrive at new facts? The sentences concerning Socrates and men are, but most others are not. Another important question is: "How does putting presuppositions together lead to a certain true conclusion?" Whether or not the relevance or sense of these questions is difficult to see depends on their foundational nature: as mentioned above, Aristotle studied the principles or rules of thinking. While Plato's models could be seen as anthropomorphosizing the dynamics of the mind, Aristotle's studies on logic appear as *formalizations of human thought processes*.

What is crucial for us is that when an idea is written on paper in the form of logical symbols, *it exists in a generalized and non-mental form*. What is so crucial about that? It does not mean anything that there is an idea on a paper—this is only significant once somebody has read the paper, and transfers the idea into her/his *mind*. But what if logic enabled us to present ideas in a form in which they could be manipulated mechanically? Aristotle's work led Pascal and Leibniz to think of this question in the seventeenth century, and to build the first mechanical calculators. Different kinds of machines were designed in the 1940s, which were able to manipulate ideas (symbols) in a much more powerful manner: digital computers. These achievements created the foundations on which the mechanical perspective of the mind was built.

*   *   *

As mentioned above, the earliest divergence point between psychoanalysis and the cognitive orientation can be traced to the Academies of Ancient Greece—Plato was the psychoanalysts' man, Aristotle a man of the cognitivists. Psychoanalytic ideas, according to which the mental unconscious consists of anthropomorphic mechanisms (inner agents) and intrapsychic conflicts, and which aim at explaining oddities of human behaviour, belong to the Platonic tradition of thought. Behind the cognitivist view of human thinking as information processing (the formalization of the thought process), interest in competencies and the (not necessarily mental) unconscious of subliminal perception, implicit memory, procedural knowledge, and algorithms (rules directing the processing of stimuli), lies Aristotle.

The Enlightenment and the mechanization of the world

The more we know about the surrounding world, the less need there is to believe in supernatural entities and to present supernatural explanations. The world of the ancient Greeks was crowded by a legion of gods, and supernatural elements had a significant role in people's world-view for the next two millennia. The Enlightenment, or the "age of reason" (1600–1800), is seen as a period when rational or scientific elements began to dominate. By jumping to the Enlightenment, I am not implying that the first fifteen centuries of our chronology are meaningless from the perspective of the development of mental terms, just that more detailed study would not serve our purposes. Anyway, there was a shift in the domain of philosophy in the seventeenth century, which is reflected in the well-known statement that modern philosophy began with Descartes. It was during that period that philosophy was transformed from a branch of theology into an independent discipline (Copleston, 1958, pp. 1–15).

The first telescopes were built at the turn of the sixteenth and seventeenth centuries. In 1610 Galileo Galilei revealed how the universe appeared through a telescope—he told of craters and mountains on the moon, the cycle of Venus, of numerous stars and galaxies. In terms of scientific progress, the seventeenth century was very successful. Some decades after Galilei's findings, Isaac Newton (1643–1727) presented his Universal Law of Gravitation, and there was progress in the domain of human anatomy, too: William Harvey discovered the circulation of blood in about 1615 (Copleston, 1958, pp. 10–11).

The seventeenth century was also a century of clocks and different kinds of mechanical automata. People were fascinated by the work of skilled clockmakers, and through them they were able to grasp how complex actions could arise from simple and concrete mechanisms. Thus, they also began to think about other things in that way—a mechanical world-view emerged. The cornerstones of that world-view were atomism, reductionism, and mathematical laws: any phenomenon could be broken down into small parts that behaved according to strict laws, and made sense of by analysing them (Channel, 1991, pp. 11–29).

From the perspective of the twenty-first century, it is difficult to see what was so new and exciting about such a world-view—in order to understand the significance of Galilei's findings, we should know the pre-Galilean way of thinking. Perhaps the most revolutionary idea was that even the stars and the universe could be studied without any immediate reference to God: the systems that drove nature, could be considered similar in principle to those that drove (mechanical) clocks, for example. Channel presents the spreading of the mechanical world-view as follows:

> At first the machine served only as analogue for biological processes; the organic world could be understood by comparison

with some well-known mechanical device or technological process. But as mechanical philosophy became successful as a method of explanation, people no longer saw a machine as simply an analogue of life—life became literally mechanical. They believed that biological processes, such as digestion, respiration, movement, and sensation, were, in fact, technological processes. [Channel, 1991, p. 30]

In the domain of physiology, the so-called *iatromechanical* (iatro = medical) movement, whose followers compared the human body with a hydraulic machine, took root in the seventeenth century (Canguilhem, 1994, pp. 93–96, 291–295; Channel, 1991, pp. 36–40). Thus, the debate on artificial intelligence and the analogy between the computer and the human mind are far from fresh—the question of whether it is reasonable to conceptualize man as a (hydraulic/ digital) machine is about 400 years old. At least in one respect the mechanical view is highly plausible: modern technology has rendered it possible to replace ill-working parts of human body, such as the heart, with mechanical devices.

Given this mechanical world-view, it is not surprising that many of the influential philosophers of the seventeenth century (Descartes, Leibniz, Pascal, Spinoza) were distinguished mathematicians. Inspired by Aristotle's ideas on logic, Blaise Pascal built mechanical apparatus that could add and subtract in 1643, and thirty-one years later Gottfried Leibniz's machine could also divide and multiply. Descartes is commonly considered the "father" of the philosophical mind–body divide and an advocate of dualism. However, he was also among those who laid the grounds for the mechanical view of man (Davis, 2000; Kreiling, 1990).

Descartes on the mind and mechanisms

René Descartes (1596–1650) and his "Cogito ergo sum" argument, according to which the only thing one can be sure of is that one thinks (or, to be precise, that thinking exists in oneself), are familiar to most of us in the West. On a more general level, Descartes presented suggestive arguments in favour of the idea that the soul was an immaterial substance. His reasoning appears intelligible to present-day people, too: if one is asked, "What is the mind", the answer "the 'mind' refers to the fact that one may possess mental images (memories) concerning matters of one's past life, entertain different ideas in one's consciousness, and make judgements on ethical matters, for instance" sounds plausible. If one knows about one philosopher it is probably Descartes, and if one is acquainted with one philosophical idea, it is very likely the "Cogito ergo sum" argument.

Descartes laid the grounds for dualistic thinking through his distinction between *res cogitans* ("a thinking thing", the mind) and *res extensia* (matter, physical objects). This philosophical distinction could be expressed as follows. Normally, we can acquire know-ledge on what a certain matter F—a lion, or a table, for example—is by trying to find some Fs and studying their common characteristics. With the mind, the situation is different, however: each person knows only her/his own. We can observe the behav-iour and reactions of other people, but their minds remain hidden to us. This is known nowadays as the "problem of other minds". Consequently, present-day philosophers and researchers of consciousness also distinguish the "first-person point of view" and the "third-person point of view". The point is that there are matters (feelings and mental images, for instance) that are accessible only to the person who possesses them; i.e., others cannot observe them from their "third-person perspective" (see, for example, Searle, 1992).

The significance of Descartes's ideas in Western culture is com-monly known, and it is not necessary to go into more detail here. What is interesting is that he also held that, for the most part, human behaviour could be explained similarly as the functioning of mech-anisms. Descartes held that mechanical explanations are plausible in the case of even quite complicated activities: the beating of the heart and the system of arteries; perceptual processes; the processing of this sense data in the imagination; remembering; the movement of the limbs; reacting to food depending on whether one is hungry or not; walking and singing (when attention is not directed to these activities). Traffic between the soul and the body is bi-directional: the soul gives orders to the body, and in the pineal gland it receives data from the bodily senses. The relation between these two sub-stances is not symmetrical: the soul possesses hegemony over the body (Cottingham, 1992, pp. 246–247; Hatfield, 1992, pp. 344–348).

In present-day terms, Descartes's view on perception could be presented as follows. The sense organs—the eyes, the receptors in the fingers and so on—form neural patterns ("ideas") of the impulses they receive. These patterns are sent to the brain (in the form of "animal spirits"), which is able to (mechanically) process this data and carry out complex activities such as those mentioned above (Rée, 1975, pp. 61–69). Instead of criticizing Descartes for his ideas on immaterial substance, one perhaps should be astonished at the sophistication of his mechanistic explanations; they are quite near to present-day cognitivist ideas of neural patterns and procedural knowledge.

The Cartesian view of the mental unconscious and censorship

Descartes studied (among other matters) the nature of the soul (mind) and the question of obtaining knowledge of its essence. In the context of the present study, it would be relevant to ask if his views can be applied to the topic of the unconscious: how should we approach the "Cartesian" questions, "Is my unconscious mental, and how could I know that?", and, "If my unconscious is mental, can I know that others' unconsciouses are mental, too?". According to the prevalent psychoanalytic view, the unconscious is capable of remembering, willing, judging, and so on (the aspects of memory, motivation, and the intellect). For Descartes, the criterion for "mentalness" was the capability to doubt one's own existence, and the unconscious does not possess that capability. Thus, in the Cartesian framework, there is no evidence that it existed apart from the body.

The significance of Descartes's thinking is also apparent in the reappearance of "Cartesian" problems in the works of later researchers: his fallacies have been difficult to avoid. The term "hidden Cartesianism" usually refers to the dualism that is implicit in one's thinking, but researchers also often face the homunculus fallacy—also in the domain of psychoanalysis.

Homunculus means "little man", and Descartes's model implies that such a being exists in the pineal gland. Neural patterns (or, in Descartes's terminology, ideas in the form of animal spirits) go from the senses to the pineal gland, and there—or through it—the soul studies them in order to make decisions about voluntary movements, for example. An ontological problem with Descartes's theory is that the soul cannot be studied scientifically. The homunculus fallacy is independent of that, however. The core of the fallacy is the following: if we explain human behaviour by assuming that there is an intelligent agent inside man, we fall into infinite regression, because then we would need to explain the "behaviour" of that agent, and so on . . .

In the domain of psychoanalysis, the problem of the homunculus fallacy is reflected in the notion of repression (Colby & Stoller, 1988, pp. 123–128). Repression is assumed to be directed towards the ideas that are in some way threatening to a person. Freud suggested in his topographical model that an agency called censorship prevented threatening ideas from entering consciousness. It appeared—like the soul in the pineal gland—in the form of a wise little man doing a complicated task. Thus, the question arose of how censorship—which is just a part of the mind/brain—could know which ideas were too threatening if they appeared in the domain of consciousness.

Leibniz, a thinking machine, and the unconscious

Fascination with mechanisms, the *zeitgeist* of the seventeenth century, led Gottfried Wilhelm Leibniz (1646–1716) to design a machine that was able to "think" in a more comprehensive manner. He never tried to build such a machine, but merely developed the project in his mind (and his writings). He reasoned that, in order to create a thinking machine, one should, first of all, be able to code true ideas concerning the world in a symbolic form. If that could be done, the same symbols could probably be presented to a machine—just as numbers and mathematical operations had been presented to the calculator that he and Pascal had built. Once this had been achieved, there should be no reason why a machine could not manipulate the symbols (just as humans manipulate ideas in their consciousness), and produce conclusions. Thus, again, we find that the basic idea of the computer and cognitive science originates in the seventeenth century, and before that in Aristotle's insight concerning logic (Copleston, 1958, pp. 264–272; Kreiling, 1990).

As mentioned above, the seventeenth century fostered the creation of entirely "mechanistic" explanations of new phenomena, such as gravitation and the functioning of the body. For us, interested in the relation between psychoanalysis and cognitive orientation, the crucial question is whether one could treat man in terms of natural science and try to create "mechanical" explanations for his essence and behaviour, and if so to what extent.

It was stated above that the idea of the unconscious as a mental entity refers to motivation, learning, imagery, memory, learning, and intellect. The tradition, which began with Aristotle, was developed by Pascal and Leibniz, and is represented by present-day researchers on artificial intelligence, offers an interesting perspective on the intellect aspect of the unconscious in that it has been shown that purely mechanical (or digital) systems are able to produce logically correct (thought) processes. The relevance of this fact has not been fully acknowledged in psychoanalytic circles.

The reason for this might lie in the fact that unconscious processes are considered as irrational, and contradictory to logic. Woody and Phillips (1995, p. 127), for example, state,

> Computational systems are ineluctably rational and normative, whereas the primary process thinking that Freud found to be characteristic of unconscious ideation is notoriously at odds with the discursive logic that is essential to both computation and information theory.

However, such a view is erroneous: so-called unconscious ideas may be false or irrational, but logic does not take a stand on the truth value of ideas. Ideas—regardless of whether they are true or not—are related to each other through rules (of at least some kind of logic). It is possible to formalize psychoanalytic ideas concerning the logic of unconscious processes ("my mother was short-tempered" + "my analyst is like my mother" = "my analyst is short-tempered", for example), and such processes may be realized in a mechanical system. Thus, in terms of the cognitivist tradition, there is no compelling reason to assume that there is anything mental behind the "intellect" of the unconscious.

As far as Leibniz is concerned, it must be admitted that he anticipated many core ideas of cognitive science (primarily computing),

and—as Tallis (2002, p. 1) puts it—also presented "the first significant entry into philosophical discussion of unconscious mental
operations". Leibniz presented his ideas on the unconscious in
the conceptual framework of *apperception, perception,* and *minute
perception.*

The term "perception" refers to any kind of experiences, or
conscious states, and, from Kant onwards, the term "apperception"
has played a significant role in philosophy and psychology.
Perception becomes apperception when it is reflected, or parts of it
are attended to. Let us think of watching a football game: one sees
the twenty-two players all the time, but it is only after reflecting on
the game, or directing one's attention to certain matters, that one
might notice the roles and characteristics of the players, or the
tactics of the teams. Thus, we could say that it is only through this
kind of thought process that perception becomes apperception.
Leibniz used the term "minute perceptions" to refer to short, or
somehow faint, sensations, which are not necessarily conscious but
nevertheless affect one's behaviour. In this he seems to have anticipated the term "subliminal perception" (Broad, 1975, pp. 130–145;
Tallis, 2002, pp. 1–4).

In the age of the Enlightenment, when the emphasis was on
mastery and control, Leibniz's ideas were unwelcome: "It was
absurd, surely, to suggest that man (equipped with 'god-like reason') should be influenced by mental events so insubstantial as to
escape his ordinary notice" (Tallis, 2002, p. 2). From the psycho-
analytical perspective, one might say that Leibniz was talking
about consciousness and pre-consciousness: the Leibnizian unconscious does not contain complex unconscious desires and fears,
but rather comprises non-attended conscious states that affect one's
behaviour.

The unconscious

In the domain of the natural sciences, certain observations make
researchers believe that there exists an entity that is not yet
known—a new particle of matter, for example—and that inspires
them to develop methods and experiments that would verify or
falsify the belief. With the mind, as well as with the unconscious, it

is a wholly different issue: ideas have developed in a continuously changing manner in Western culture. According to Whyte (1960, p. 15) the development of mental terms should be comprised in thinking whether a certain idea was *conceivable*, *topical*, or *effective* for the people living in a certain era. Account should also be taken of whether the idea was conceivable to ordinary people, or to those who had the time and interest to speculate on, say, "metaphysical" issues. In this sense, we might state that the idea of the immaterial mind/soul was conceivable for some men in Hellenistic societies in the pre-Socratic era, it has been relevant to many Western people since the emergence of the Christian religion, and it is effective in all present-day Western cultures. How about the unconscious?

Whyte's conception of it becomes more complex. The term unconscious refers to matters of which one cannot make sense and that cannot be controlled. At first, those non-controllable, alien matters—the "oddities"—were explained in terms of supernatural outward stories that have later turned to more or less psychological inward ones. However, the term unconscious has not always been part of those inward stories—Leibniz, among others, may be said to have studied the unconscious, although the term was not used in his day.

The roots of the Western idea of the unconscious as "an intangible 'thing' that the human being possesses" lie in Homer's poems: the unconscious appears as an internal mechanism that receives the wishes of the gods (Claxton, 2005, p. 61). We should remember that "oddities of human behaviour and experience" have been explained in different ways in the course of history, and the term "unconscious" refers to recent non-supernatural, or at least *less* supernatural, means of explanation. According to Claxton (2005, p. 22), "Explicit conceptualizing of unconscious mental states needed a well-developed notion of the mind as 'the organ of intelligence' to hook onto . . ." (see also Whyte, 1960, pp. 59–76).

In English literature, the idea that one might be unconscious of one's own mental process dates back to the year 1751. The German terms *Unbewusstsein* and *Bewusstlos* were also used in that century for the first time—according to Whyte (1960, p. 116), Platner (1744–1818) was the first to use them. The term *inconsciente* appeared in French a hundred years later (in the 1850s). Thus, the idea of unconscious ideas or desires has been accessible through the major

Western languages for less than 300 hundred years (Whyte, 1960, pp. 66–67).

We can, thus, compute the era during which the idea of the unconscious became explicit to Europeans: according to Tallis (2002, p. 5), ". . . right from the beginning, the existence of the unconscious was fully accepted and integrated into romantic psychology", and Claxton (2005, p. 153) suggested that the romantic movement "rekindled, developed and began to give explicit voice to several varieties of the unconscious that had been implicit in human culture from the dawn of history".

Freud was a child of romanticism. The era covered approximately a century prior to his first psychoanalytic writings, and, in comparison with the writings of Pierre Janet and Alfred Adler, Freud's (and especially Jung's) ideas were characteristically romantic in tone (Ellenberger, 1970, pp. 887–888). While the era of the Enlightenment was preoccupied with machines and rationality, romanticism focused on wholly different matters: dreams, mystical experiences, mesmerism/hypnosis, and nature. Thus, and not surprisingly, the unconscious was a very popular topic in the nineteenth century—philosophers (Schopenhauer, Nietzsche) as well as novelists (Dostoevsky) embraced it, and books such as *The Philosophy of the Unconscious* (von Hartman, 1869) and *Symbolism of Dreams* (von Schubert, 1814) were published. There is even a connection between romanticism and the 1960s and flower-power: drugs (opium) were sometimes seen as a route to the unconscious (Claxton, 2005, pp. 120–154; Tallis, 2002, pp. 16–34).

Dipsychism and polypsychism

Two views of the unconscious were prevalent in the era of romanticism: dipsychism and polypsychism (Ellenberger, 1970, pp. 145–147; Tallis, 2002, p. 28). According to the former, the unconscious is like a double ego, a second personality ("under consciousness") with similar competencies to the conscious ego ("upper consciousness"). Tallis describes polypsychism through the metaphor of a classical orchestra: the unconscious contains "lesser minds" that resemble sections of the orchestra (stringed, wind, and brass instruments).

It is through this distinction that the essential differences between the psychoanalytic and the cognitive unconscious can also be made visible. Apart from in his early writings with Breuer, Freud's view on unconscious motives and (Platonic) internal agents such as censorship clearly fell on the side of dipsychism. The roots of the polypsychist view lie in Aristotle's studies on mental operations, but it was Leibniz who laid the grounds for that view on the unconscious, which preceded cognitivist ideas on the modularity of the mind, parallel distributed processes, and implicit knowledge. Thus, within the cognitive orientation, the unconscious is seen in terms of different kinds of unconscious processes and behavioural dispositions, which are not as sophisticated as Freudian presuppositions of unconscious ideas and mental agencies. Currently, the dipsychism–polypsychism distinction appears in the debates on whether the unconscious is "wise or dumb" (see, for instance, Haskell, 2003), and on whether the lack of contents in consciousness should be conceptualized in terms of repression or dissociation.

Dipsychism cannot avoid falling into the trap of the homunculus fallacy, and polypsychism faces that danger, too: how those "lesser minds" (modular activity or implicit memory systems of the brain) are "orchestrated" in order to produce the phenomena that psychoanalysts face in their practice. Within the cognitive orientation, this problem is seen in terms of self-organization and non-linear dynamics, for example.

*   *   *

The Aristotelian/Leibnizian polypsychist tradition of thinking constitutes the cognitive orientation, but for psychoanalysis its "mathematical" flavour is alien. Matte-Blanco's (1975) *The Unconscious as Infinite Sets* is a monumental counter-example, and Colby's (1981) computer model of the paranoid mind and Lloyd's (1998) study on Freud's Lucy R should also be mentioned as groundbreaking exceptions. In his book *The Emergent Ego: Complexity and Coevolution in the Psychoanalytic Process*, Stanley Palombo (1999) considers the psychoanalytic process in terms of non-linear dynamics. This is a work that should enjoy the reputation of being the most challenging psychoanalytic writing since *The Interpretation of Dreams*, but "Aristotelian" viewpoints are far from the focus of psychoanalysts' interests. Submitting a manuscript applying the computer metaphor to a psychoanalytic journal more often than not provokes emotional reactions from reviewers.

In the domain of empirical study of the unconscious there is, nevertheless, an interesting connection between psychoanalytic and cognitive traditions. Namely, in the scope of psychoanalysis, subliminal stimuli have been used since 1917, when Otto Pötzl flashed pictures subliminally to subjects and requested them to have a dream. He aimed to show that subliminally presented stimuli could appear in dreams. In terms of the standards of present-day science, Pötzl's experiments were far from sophisticated, but they nevertheless gave rise to a tradition of research. Pötzl was a member of the Vienna Psychoanalytic Society, and Freud was fascinated by his studies. It was through the later works of Charles Fisher (from the 1950s onwards) and Lloyd Silverman (from the 1970s onwards) that there emerged a tradition of research focusing on subliminal psychodynamic activation (SPA) (Bornstein, 1990, pp. 62–63; Erdelyi, 1996, pp. 72–81).

The main idea behind SPA is that subliminal stimuli bypass ego defences, and thus are able to activate unconscious conflicts. Silverman presented subjects subliminally with sentences such as "Mommy and I are one", "Mommy is leaving me", and "Beating dad is wrong", which were targeted to tap certain oedipal or oral unconscious fantasies. In one of his best known experiments (Silverman, Ross, Adler, & Lustig, 1978) he presented his subjects with a message that increased their anxiety related to oedipal conflict ("Beating dad is wrong"), decreased it ("Beating dad is OK"), or was neutral ("People are standing"). It was found that, in a dart-throwing competition, anxiety-increasing messages lowered the scores, anxiety-decreasing messages improved performance, and neutral messages did not affect it (Bornstein, 1990; Silverman, 1983).

Researchers have, however, disagreed about the results of SPA studies. Silverman (1983, p. 90) claimed that, of the studies in which *he had not participated*, thirty-four had supported SPA, thirteen had mixed results, and eight were clearly non-supportive. Fudin (1999, p. 235), for his part, concluded that

> ... none of his [Silverman's] experiments can be replicated, and ... no experiment using Silverman's procedures can yield unambiguous positive results ...

Freud and the unconscious

As we see, contrary to a prevalent claim, Sigmund Freud did not "found" the unconscious, and his contribution was not wholly original either—he learned from his contemporaries Friedrich Nietzsche and Arthur Schopenhauer more than he was willing to admit. Charcot also used the notion of the unconscious for clinical purposes before Freud. Zaretsky (2004, pp. 15–40) argues that Freud's ideas on the unconscious differed from those of his contemporaries (and predecessors) in that he thought of it as *personal*: "an internal, idiosyncratic source of motivations peculiar to the individual" (*ibid.*, p. 16). It was Freud who created a consistent system through which human behaviour could be interpreted in terms of unconscious aims and memories, and with the help of which psychic disorders could be treated.

Freud wrote in German, and the essential "mental" terms in that language are *Seele/seelische, Psyche/psychische* and *Geist/geistig. Seele* is usually translated as "soul", but its origin differs from that of the English word: *Seele* originates in the word *See*, ocean. *Geist* has a Gothic origin, and it is usually translated as "mind", "spirit", or "intellect". Interestingly, when the word "mental" appears in the English translations of Freud's writings, the original word is often *Seele* (Bettelheim, 1982, pp. 70–78; Grimm & Grimm, 1897).

Bettelheim (1982) gave his well-known critique of the standard English translation of Freud's works in his book *Freud and Man's Soul*. According to him, it was a serious error to translate *Seele/seelisch* as "mind-mental"—"soul" would have been better. In the context of the present study, it is of particular relevance which word—*Seele*, "psyche" or *Geist*—Freud used to emphasize the mental essence of the unconscious. The sentence, "It is clear in any case that this question—whether the latent states of mental life, whose existence is undeniable, are to be conceived of as conscious mental states or as physical ones . . ." (Freud 1915e, p. 168) was written in German as follows: "Immerhin ist es klar, dass die Frage, ob man die unabweisbaren latent Zustande des *Seelenlebens* als unbewusste *seelische* oder als physische auffassen soll . . ." (Freud 1915e, p. 266, my italics). Was it the case that Freud referred to different matters when he used the word *seelisch* on the one hand and *psychisch* on the other? Should we replace the idea of the mental unconscious by speaking about the unconscious soul?

Freud was a "militant" atheist (Gay, 1987, p. 37), and his view on the unconscious certainly did not incorporate any hidden religious agenda. At the time of Freud's birth in the middle of the nineteenth century, romanticism was turning into scientism and positivism (Galdston, 1956). Thus, we cannot claim either that he based his view of the nature of the unconscious on the philosophy of science, which is entirely alien to the present-day scientists.

Thus, we might legitimately assume that, in referring to the mental/*seelisch* unconscious, Freud did not mean anything mystical, or anything that would imply dualism—he did not aim at presenting a supernatural explanation. All this makes it difficult to understand why he emphasized the mental nature of the unconscious, and what he meant by the term *Seele/seelisch*. What is particularly confusing is that *Seele does* have a religious connotation in German, and that Freud the atheist–materialist deliberately used that term.

Bettelheim (1982, pp. 76–77) offered some ideas for clearing up this confusion. According to him, Freud (often) preferred *Seele* over *Geist* because the latter term refers to rational aspects of the mind, and the emphasis in psychoanalysis is on the non-rational. He noted that Freud never gave a precise definition for *Seele*, and thought this was not by chance: Freud used the term "*because* of its inexactitude, its emotional resonance."

"What Freud really said/meant" discussions usually contain the presupposition that, contrary to other people, Freud always had a clear image of what he was trying to say. It is, however, fruitful to study his idea of the mental essence of the unconscious from the other angle—perhaps he had a problem that he was unable to solve. Maybe even Freud himself did not know what would it mean that the unconscious is mental. Let us collect the facts supporting this hypothesis.

First, if Freud had known what he meant by the claim that the unconscious is mental, he would have said that. However, he was never clear with that, and he remained ambiguous about whether the unconscious becomes reduced to neurophysiological matters. Second, he also had not used both the words *psychische* and *seelische* in order to describe the unconscious—he would have avoided the latter because of its religious connotations. Third, if he had a clear idea on the mentalness of the unconscious, Freud would have studied it in a detailed manner from the perspective of Brentano's view concerning intentionality.

For Freud, the mental essence of the unconscious was the cornerstone of psychoanalysis. In so far as he had good arguments in favour of that claim, he would not have hesitated to express them. In order to reach what might have been the problem that Freud aimed to solve with the idea of the mental essence of the unconscious, let us look more closely into his intellectual background.

The mental unconscious: the tension between romantic roots and scientific ideals

Freud's thinking had romantic undertones in many respects. The essential "Freudian" topics of hypnosis, the interpretation of dreams, sexuality, and fantasy, as well as his interdisciplinary approach (psychology, anthropology, studies on the arts, and neurophysiology), clearly reflect that spirit. Many of his favourite poets (Goethe, Schiller) and philosophers (Nietzsche, Schopenhauer) also had a romantic streak. (Cranefield, 1966a,b; Ellenberger, 1970, pp. 534–542; Galdston, 1956).

There was also a touch of romanticism among Freud's close friends and colleagues. Wilhelm Fliess was the most influential of these, and Freud always presented his ideas first to him. Fliess himself had interests that were very far from those of Freud, numerology and biorythms being among them. Galdston (1956, pp. 495–502) suggested that it was through Fliess that the ideas of romanticism found their way into Freud's works. Freud also had serious discussions on mystical topics with Jung (Sulloway, 1979, pp. 135–237).

Freud's use of mechanical metaphors on the mind–brain could be seen as a reflection of the Enlightenment fascination with mechanical apparatus. However, there are romantic roots behind even some technically-sounding terms.

Gustav Fechner is considered a great figure in the history of psychology, known for his "psychophysical law", and Freud also respected him highly. According to Ellenberger (1970, p. 542), the concept of mental energy, the principles of pleasure–unpleasure, constancy and repetition, and the topographic model of the mind, all derive from Fechner. Fechner's roots were deep in romanticism: under the pseudonym of Dr Mishes, he wrote the pamphlet "Comparative anatomy of angels", and he tried to reconcile the laws of the spiritual and physical worlds. At that time the romantic philosophy of nature was already old-fashioned, and because of that he presented his ideas within the conceptual framework of experimental psychology (Copleston, 1963, pp. 375–376; Ellenberger, 1970, pp. 215–218).

The "mesmerism" of the nineteenth century, later called hypnosis, was the "basic approach to the unconscious mind" (Ellenberger, 1970, p. 120). The realm of hypnosis was a major battleground, or, as a matter of fact, two battlegrounds. There was heated debate on supernatural explanations on the one hand: Ellenberger (1970, p. 53) traced the emergence of dynamic psychiatry to the year 1775, when the exorcist Johann Gassner's supernatural explanation for certain oddities was surpassed by that of Franz Mesmer (1734–1815).

On the other hand, there were conflicting views on hidden fluids and forces. Mesmer explained the effectiviness of his treatment in terms of an invisible fluid he called "animal magnetism" (the term refers, again, to the soul, the anima). Interestingly, in this case physiological explanation came first, but the fluid was never identified, and researchers began to offer psychological explanations. Freud was very well informed on the notion of animal magnetism, because that line of explanation persisted along with the psychological ones during the entire nineteenth century (Drinka, 1984, pp. 123–151; Ellenberger, 1970, p. 148).

Freud adopted his scientific ideals from the so-called "school of Helmholtz", which included Emil du Bois-Reymond, Ernst Brücke, Carl Ludvig, and Hermann Helmholtz, and which strongly contradicted the spirit of romanticism (or "German idealism"). He began his scientific studies in the domain of physiology, and studied eels and the effects of cocaine, among other things. However, for economic reasons, he decided to abandon that career, and began to work as a clinician. By the middle of the nineteenth century the "school of Helmholtz" had sketched the basics of neurological thinking, which was later encapsulated in the terms "(naive) reductionism", "sterile scientism", "mechanistic", and "positivistic".

When Freud was studying medicine at the end of the century, its impact had already decreased, although it is often claimed that, through his teachers Brücke, Theodor Meynert, and Sigmund Exnert, he adopted rather reductionist scientific ideals (Cranefield, 1966b; Ellenberger, 1970, p. 535; Gay, 1988, pp. 32–37).

The tension between romantic interest and reductionist philosophical presupposition in Freud's thinking has often been noted (e.g., Cranefield 1966b; Galdston, 1956; Holt, 1989, pp. 31–33). Below, I focus on this tension, from which his ideas on the unconscious arose.

The phenomena that led Freud to stress the mental essence of the unconscious included the following: people, without conscious planning, create fantasies, psychic disorders, associations, metaphors, and dreams, which symbolically present intrapsychic conflicts; the human brain is capable of anticipating distressing situations (by prohibiting the formation of certain contents of consciousness); and the human capability to detect dangerous/ distressing situations without conscious thinking (stimuli triggering psychic disorders). Freud also noticed interrelations between his patients' disorders, slips of the tongue, dreams, life-histories, hidden memories, and their reactions towards himself (transference). These interrelations were not present by chance—he was inclined to think that they had, or served, some purpose.

These notions would have been easy to comprehend, given the interests of young Freud in German idealism, but because of his scientific ideals he did not wish to present his ideas in such a terminological framework. On the other hand, he could not explain his notions in terms of the "school of Helmholtz" either. Galdston presented that impossibility as follows:

> Intentions and purposes smacked of vitalism, and reeked of teleology. Life, according to prevailing scientific belief, was to be accounted for in terms of matter and energy, in terms of molecules in motion. Purpose and intention had neither place nor meaning in the realm of science. [Galdston, 1956, p. 494]

According to Holt (1989, p. 352), Freud's ". . . theories were always more or less successful struggles to synthesize the themes and outlook of humanism with those of mechanistic metaphysics".

On these grounds, we might understand the idea of the mental unconscious as a "compromise formation" between Freud's romantic background, his clinical observations, and the (reductionist) ideal of science he had adopted. In those times the term "mental" (*seelische, psychische*), as it appeared to Freud, was perhaps the best one to describe the unconscious.

"Psychic energy" and "an unconscious idea" are matters that cannot be perceived through senses or measures. A present-day neuroscientist aiming at explaining human behaviour through a not-yet-discovered substance would be seen as a dualist presenting a supernatural explanation. However, the situation was different at the end of 1800s; people felt more free to speculate. Isaac Newton's mechanics has been considered an exemplar for Freud's metapsychology, but, according to Gay (1988, pp. 79–80), Freud followed the great Newton in other ways, too: Newton held that, although gravity remained invisible, it was worth studying. Freud applied that view to psychic energy and unconscious mental contents. It is also worth mentioning that Kant and Hegel were the great philosophers of Freud's youth, and both of them were of the opinion that it was not the real state of things that we perceive by our senses—there are matters that exist even though they cannot be perceived. Freud's friend, Ludwig Binswanger, spoke of a discussion (see Fichtner, 1992, p. 237) in which Freud (inaccurately) claimed that the unconscious might be equated to Kant's "thing in itself".

It is surprising and unfortunate that Freud did not clarify his relation to Franz Brentano (1838–1917). Brentano held that intentionality—the fact that conscious states refer to what is outside of individuals differently than pictures do—makes the difference between the mental and the material. Along with Brentano's studies, the term intentionality has become a concept that cannot be overlooked in studies of the nature of the mind and the essence of the mental. Freud attended Brentano's lectures and, indeed, respected him highly (Gay, 1988, pp. 29–31). Although Brentano's ideas were extremely relevant to the debate on the mental nature of the unconscious, Freud quoted him just once in his works (a short footnote in *Jokes and Their Relation to the Unconscious*, 1905c).

Thus, we know that first, he had no sympathies toward dualistic lines of thought, and second, he was *very* eager to explain phenomena in terms of neurophysiology. What should we, on these grounds, think about the mental essence of the unconscious? I think the following conclusion should be drawn: Freud's clinical observations (symbolism in dreams and disorders, for example) indicated that the unconscious is flexible, in a certain way very "clever", and, say, creative. Freud could not *even conceive* of how such observations could be explained in terms of neuroscience—that was rather reductionistic and mechanical at that time.

From that perspective, emphasis on "mental" should not be understood in terms of the mind–matter dichotomy. Instead, the dichotomy inert matter–living organism is more plausible: for Freud, the brain was too mechanical a system to give rise to phenomena he found.

*   *   *

According to Kitcher, psychoanalysis developed as an interdisciplinary theory, and she holds that Freud's hypotheses "enjoyed a substantial amount of support by nineteenth-century standards" (Kitcher, 1992, pp. 109–110). However, from the present-day perspective Freud's ideas appear otherwise:

> He [Freud] relied too much on the smooth progress of neurophysiology, took much too great risk in hoping that physiology would provide an adequate grounding for libido theory, and was overly impressed by the potential unity of his theory of mental to see that real connections had to be made, not simply assumed. [*ibid.*, p. 182]

We might say that Freud's emphasis on the mental essence of the unconscious should be seen through the question of *how to talk about matters that cannot be observed*. Foundations of neurophysiology, for example, have not changed since Freud's times, but the above question is nowadays approached wholly differently. Freud attempted to explain the apparent goal-directness of the unconscious several decades before von Bertalanffy's ideas on systems, Shannon's cybernetics, evolutionary biologists' ideas on functions, the concept of non-linear dynamics, and philosophers' conceptions of "as-if" intentionality emerged.

CHAPTER THREE

The mind and the unconscious of the post-Freudian era

H istories of science used to focus on Ancient Greece and the seventeenth century, and those periods possessed the key role when the unconscious was studied from the perspective of history of ideas in the previous chapter. At the beginning of the chapter I cited Paul Macdonald stating the core problem with the history of the concept "mind": there is no consensus on what the concept of mind picks out or to what it makes reference. When seen from the historical perspective, mental concepts appear to have been connected to, first, mysteries, which later have been withdrawn due to the development of science. Second, they are intimately related to certain religious and theological ideas and ideals. According to present-day layman intuition, possessing a mind means simply that there are feelings and mental images in the scope of one's consciousness (perhaps some people might also mention matters like the ability to feel guilty).

That intuition reflects the era we live in: the mystery of the mind has narrowed, its supernatural resonance has abated, and the reference of mental terms has become focused on the phenomenal qualities of experience. To put this in philosophical jargon, in the core of mind–body problem there is the *problem of qualia*.

We might say that modern philosophy of mind both started from Descartes's *cogito ergo sum* argument, and remained its prisoner: Descartes gave a form for the mind–body problem, and present-day philosophers, neuroscientists, and psychologists still wrestle with his conceptualization. The problem can be stated in many ways, and I think the following down-to-earth way best serves our purposes.

Apart from some philosophers (when talking technically), all humans confess to possessing feelings such as pain and pleasure. We also have mental images in the scope of our consciousness; we have perceptions on the surrounding world, and fantasies about matters that might or might not take place in real life, and we relive past events in our memories. The philosophers' expressions "qualitative aspect of consciousness" and "phenomenal consciousness" refer to these matters.

Phenomenal consciousness is felt and noticed only by a person him- or herself, but we are compelled to think that other people have it also, and at least those people who have pets cannot escape from thinking that many animals possess it, too. Phenomenal consciousness makes the difference between creatures that have and do not have a mind; just a few people think that rocks, robots, and computers might possess phenomenal consciousness, and thus a mind.

There is no commonly accepted theory on how the material world gave rise to the first phenomenal consciousness on earth, and how millions of minds emerge from biological structures and processes every day. Because of that, mind and phenomenal consciousness is a mystery for present-day science.

The mind–body problem reflects tensions between our layman intuitions and scientific (materialistic) ideas. Philosophers' work is to challenge layman intuitions, and a philosopher would point out that the existence of phenomenal consciousness cannot be observed objectively from the third-person perspective. Essentially, strictly speaking, we cannot know for sure that someone possesses phenomenal consciousness—perhaps the person is a zombie who just produces sentences like "I'm in pain". When someone claims that we should accept verbal reports as a proof for phenomenal consciousness, he or she should be asked if a computer's report on its internal state should be taken as such a proof.

It may be difficult for a non-philosopher to make sense of this kind of argument challenging our common sense. However, philosophers have to reflect the reliability of subjective reports from a more general perspective. If we accept subjective reports as a proof of the existence of mental (i.e., non-material) entities, should we not also accept them as a proof of the existence of gods, or unobservable energies and forces, about which people claim to have had experiences? From the scientific perspective, leaning or not leaning on our personal experiences is a question of principle.

There is also the layman intuition that mental matters cause bodily movements—a plan or a feeling of pain are seen as capable of making one's arm move, for example. From the scientific perspective such an idea is as unintelligible as the one that we might make a chair move across a room by our mental powers (psychokinesis). For most people it is easy to see that the latter case means that a physical object would move without a physical cause, and that such a state of things would violate the laws of nature (and thus challenge the views of natural science). In principle, however, the situation is the same with the former case: the claim that a non-material entity like the feeling of pain or a mental image makes one's body move challenges the world-view of natural sciences as well.

A philosopher advocating the above layman intuitions is considered dualistic, and in our times an ambitious philosopher does not want to appear as such. Thus, they propose solutions for the mind–body problem (and argue that their colleagues' proposals are, after all, dualistic). There are two main strategies in those proposals. First, one may (try to) deny that there is anything mental in the world. The fruits of this strategy are to be set under the label "eliminative materialism". Patricia Churchland (2002) has suggested that the mystery around the mind should be seen as similar to those that once surrounded electricity and epileptic seizures, for example: although a supernatural or dualistic explanation may seem intuitively plausible, researchers will some day give us a physical explanation.

Second, one may argue that phenomenal consciousness is just an aspect of materia, or an emergent property of it. One may dispute whether it sounds more absurd to claim that a feeling of pain does not exist, or that it is actually an aspect of materia (see John Searle's and Daniel Searle's debate in Chapter Five of Searle's book *The Mystery of Consciousness* [Searle, 1997]). Anyway, those who try to say that mental matters are basically material call themselves emergent materialists, or monists. This second strategy is "realist", i.e., respects our common-sense view.

Let us emphasize that the mind–body problem has not been solved in the scope of it—calling oneself an emergent materialist or a monist presents just one's opinion on how the problem should be addressed. We might say that when a layman sincerely shares his or her intuition concerning mind, body, and their relationship, the result is a dualistic view that might, however, easily be camouflaged as emergent materialism or monism.

I have reviewed the present-day status of the mind–body problem in a concise and slightly laconic manner, because it is not reasonable to probe (even) deeper into it. (A reader who would like to read more about the topic might study the books of, for example, Dennett, Searle, Paul and Patricia Churchland, Jaegwon Kim, and Thomas Nagel.)

When a researcher is interested in, for example, autism, psychology behind traffic accidents, chess-playing, psychic disorders, or learning disabilities, there are many scientific problems. The philosophical mind–body problem always lurks behind a behavioural scientist, but taking an explicit stance towards it does not enable him or her to solve the scientific problems. Quite contrary: if the researcher's model is based on a certain philosophical attitude towards the mind–body problem, suspicions arise—how might a certain (controversial) attitude toward the mystery of the mind shed light on the topic? A researcher would be in danger of slipping into an endless philosophical debate that might overshadow his or her insights. Actually, it would sound very odd to say "Our studies on autism are based on Sir John Eccles' dualistic view", or "Behind our model on learning disabilities there is Paul Churchland's eliminative materialism".

A researcher has to decide if he or she is doing philosophy or science. When the latter (and also a specific topic) become chosen, researchers lean on the layman intuitions presented above—humans' just possess feelings, memories, fantasies, beliefs, and so on. It is simply held that the term "mind" refers to phenomenal consciousness and characteristics of conscious states. When a researcher uses the term "mental" otherwise, usually there are no specific philosophical principles behind that.

The above should hold with psychoanalytically orientated researchers, too. In the focus of psychoanalysis there are also observations on phenomenal and behavioural facts that the analysts have made of their analysands, and each of us has made on him- or herself. It is common knowledge that we often, for example, forget significant matters, deny desires and fears that we clearly appear to possess, and do not recognize being envious or angry although our behaviour and expression indicate that we are. In the scope of psychoanalysis, these phenomena are approached in terms of the unconscious, censorship, repression, and resistance. All in all, it is hard to see any foundational difference between the psychoanalytic interest and the interests of the researchers studying the psychology of traffic accidents or chess-playing.

As we know, however, psychoanalytically orientated people are deeply involved in the Freudian view that the term mind refers also to non-phenomenal matters. This means that there is a *foundational* disagreement between psychoanalysis and present-day cognitive neuroscience. Below, that disagreement is articulated in terms of the two-sphere and three-sphere views. The former represents the approach of cognitive neuroscience, according to which man should be studied in terms of two spheres: phenomenal consciousness (which is seen as equivalent with the term "mind") on the one hand, and the structures and processes of the brain on the other. In the scope of psychoanalysis, it has been thought of in terms of three spheres: consciousness (the conscious part of the mind), the unconscious (the unconscious part of the mind), and the brain.

Below, I first present the logic behind the two-sphere view, and then we turn to study how the three-sphere view appeared in our times—more than a century after Freud sketched it. At the end of the 1990s the endeavour of neuro-psychoanalysis emerged, which—as the name indicates—approaches psychoanalytic issues from the perspective of neuroscience. It is crucial to find out which view it depends on. Thus, that matter is the focus of the closing section of the chapter.

The two-sphere view and its foundations

Frank Tallis gives the impression that mid-twentieth-century advances in neuroscience caused an anti-Cartesian revolution:

In the 1930s and 1940s the Canadian neurosurgeon Wilder Penfield conducted an extraordinary series of experiments that dramatically demonstrated the intimate relationship between brain and mind. His work represented a troubling challenge to the advocates of Cartesian dualism. The 1.4 kg of gelatinous matter that comprises the human brain was shown to be the organ of consciousness—the physical reality behind the phenomenal world. [Tallis, 2002, p. 110]

Penfield, originally studying epileptic seizures, stimulated patients' brains with an electric probe, and that produced specific responses: depending on which area of the brain was stimulated, patients heard clicks, felt hot or cold, and had *déjà vu* experiences or visual and auditory hallucinations. Actually, Penfield's findings were not as clear as they appeared (Squire & Kandel, 1999, p. 11), but nevertheless they seriously challenged Cartesian intuitions. According to Kandel (2005, p. 40), the idea that all mental functions reflect the functions of the brain is nowadays "almost a truism".

Another classical series of experiments was that conducted by Benjamin Libet. He was able to show that "readiness potential" (RP) occurred 220–550 msec before the conscious *decision* to move one's finger. Thus, "*initiation* of the voluntary process is developed unconsciously, well before there is any awareness of intention to act" (Libet, 1996, p. 112; original emphasis). Descartes held that the soul gave orders to the body, but, in the light of Libet's experiments, it appears that the opposite is the case: neurophysiological machinery of the brain creates conscious states. Experiments conducted by Libet and others have given rise to the idea that consciousness in itself could be considered an illusion, just a side-product of neural activity (see Dennett 2003; Wegner, 2002). Thus, in the scope of present-day cognitive science there is no doubt that unconscious matters determine our behaviour—it is the role of consciousness that is in question.

It is as a result of this kind of neuroscientific study that the relations between the body/brain and various mental concepts (the mind, consciousness, awareness) have become less complex. There seem to be just two spheres or levels—the neurophysiological (the body–brain), and conscious states (feelings, mental images, and so on). There is no need to talk about unconscious *mental* matters—the term "unconscious" merely refers to brain processes.

Thus, among scientists and philosophers there is currently consensus that the brain directs the mind, or consciousness, or at least that it emerges from the neurophysiological processes. There is, however, no generally accepted theory on how or why that is the case: the mind/consciousness/intentionality is still a mystery.

Cognitive (neuro)science, or the cognitive orientation—the mainstream of present-day behavioural sciences—began to emerge in the 1940s. That was when the first computers were built, and researchers found them a useful tool in the study of the human mind/brain. The year 1956 is considered significant in the history of the cognitive orientation, because it was then that an inspirational seminar was held in MIT, in which the leading researchers of the field participated. It was not until two or three decades later, however, that the term "cognitive science" came into common usage. Nowadays, cognitive (neuro)science means a paradigm of research, or a loose basic orientation that is applicable in several domains of study, including psychology, philosophy, linguistics, anthropology, computer science, and neurophysiology.

It is only after having become acquainted with the findings of post-war neuroscience that one can understand the significance of the so-called "computer metaphor" to the cognitive orientation. If the brain is considered "the organ of consciousness"—as Tallis puts it—there is no need to suppose that there are any "animal" substances or forces between consciousness and the brain. It is through this kind of logic that the mystery of the mind takes the form of the question, "Which properties of the brain cause, or give rise to consciousness?" In a world filled with computers capable of performing many human-like functions, it is reasonable to approach this question by asking another: why do computers not exhibit consciousness, and could they do so one day?

Studying the human mind/brain from the Aristotelian/ Leibnizian perspective—in terms of information processing, neural algorithms, computations, neural representations, and rules of thought—has been useful in two ways. For philosophers, the computer metaphor provided a fresh perspective on the age-old mind–body problem, while it has been a concrete tool for scientists: it has been possible to test theories and models by creating computer simulations. The metaphor has also provided cognitive insights into intentionality—a subject Freud became familiar with in Brentano's lectures.

In the eighteenth century, laymen began to think of human essence in terms of mechanical metaphors, and two centuries later the computer metaphor became part of our "folk psychology". Let us take an example of the latter from Rich Cohen's book, *The Record Men: Chess Records and The Birth of Rock & Roll*, that portrays the collaboration between record companies and musicians in the 1950s and 1960s. In it we find "a record man" describing the difference between musicians and themselves as follows:

> Assume the human brain is made of chips like a computer. And those chips govern behavior. Well, these [musicians] can take a sheet of paper and put notes on it and go into a studio and translate it into music and perform that music in front of millions. We can't do that. They got chips we don't. But to make room for those chips, other chips fall out. Sanity, reason, logic, gratitude. Anything like that is gone. [Cohen, 2005, 123–124]

Intrinsic and as-if intentionality

As mentioned in Chapter Two, it was through Brentano's writings at the end of the nineteenth century that the term intentionality came to the fore in the philosophy of the mind. Intentionality is a technical term, and is not derived from the words "intention" or "intend": it refers to *aboutness*. Aboutness characterizes humans' mental life: our perceptions, dreams, and memories are about things outside us, and our fears and desires are directed to certain objects or matters. The core idea behind human intentionality is that mental states refer to what is outside of individuals themselves.

I should add at once that physical entities also refer to what is outside of themselves: a photograph of Paris and the sentence "Paris is a beautiful city" are about Paris and refer to it. Computers also function in a manner that resembles humans' goal-directed behaviour arising from fears and desires: they aim at certain things ("desire"; to keep their clocks at the right time, for instance), and try to avoid others ("fear"; to protect themselves from virus infections). Plants, too, seem to strive for objects: they frequently turn towards the sun, for example. Thus, present-day cognitive science does not presuppose that only humans possess intentionality: the epithet "intrinsinc" (or "original") is used for human intentionality, and "as-if" (or derived) often precedes the term when it is talked about in connection with pictures, computers, or plants (see, for example, Dennett & Haugeland, 1998; Searle, 1992, pp. 78–82).

The mind–body problem often appears through the term intentionality. When an author holds that original intentionality is wholly different from as-if intentionality, he/she is often accused of hidden Cartesianism. Not surprisingly, the eliminative materialist usually does not see any fundamental difference between the two.

In the scope of this work, all this means that the claim "The unconscious is mental in essence" is (almost) identical to the claim "The unconscious possesses original intentionality". Thus, if the latter holds, the unconscious is mental in essence. Similarly, if the "competencies" of the unconscious (which is why Freud called it mental) turn out to be based on as-if intentionality, it is difficult to see why the unconscious should be considered mental.

In terms of the conventional conception of intentionality, the answer is in the definition: humans' intrinsic intentionality comes from the fact that *conscious states*, as we experience them, are about something. Because unconscious states are not experienced, and they do not—of course—appear in the scope of consciousness, the unconscious is not intentional. Thus, in terms of intentionality, the idea of mental unconscious is an oxymoron, and probably that is the reason why Freud never reflected (in public) his ideas in the light of Brentano's thinking.

The study of repressed desires and fears is essentially about behaviour that appears as goal-orientated. In order to make sense of when such behaviour should be seen as intrinsically intentional, intentionality is classified below as mechanical, biological, or mental. The study is based on contemporary views (for example, Dennett & Haugeland, 1998; Searle 1992, pp. 78–82), but it was inspired by Dennett (for instance, 1978, pp. 3–58, 233–285).

Let us begin by thinking of the behaviour of flowers turning towards the sun. They do that every morning, and Daniel wakes up early one morning and does the same (because that morning there is a partial eclipse of the sun). We could also imagine a solar panel system turning towards the sun: there is a censor detecting sunbeams, and a computer turning the panel towards the sun according to the information received from the censor. Thus, we find goal-directed, turning-towards-the-sun behaviour in flowers, Daniel, and the solar panel. In Daniel's case there is intrinsic, mental intentionality: his consciousness contains beliefs ("There will be an eclipse of the sun in the morning") and desires ("I want to see the eclipse of the sun") about the sun. There is no intrinsic intentionality in the solar panel: it detects sunbeams and turns towards the sun just because a computer engineer has programmed it to do so. It has been assumed that mechanical intentionality in computers is derived from the programmer: he or she possessed intrinsic intentionality when building the programme, and the programme's intentionality is thus derived (hence, the term "derived intentionality" is used as synonym for as-if intentionality). We could also say that the engineer possessed mental goal-directedness, whereas the solar panel system is goal-directed in a mechanical manner.

Consequently, the flower is goal-directed in a biological manner: sunbeams cause biological processes that make it turn towards the sun. In this case, the behaviour is driven by the logic of evolution: it became prevalent millions of years ago in the interests of survival. Dennett is used to say that the "behaviour" of plants and animals—turning towards the sun is one example—was "designed by mother nature", and thus biological intentionality derives from her. In this he is suggesting that such acts are not arbitrary, but arise from the logic of evolution.

The above picture of mental, biological, and mechanical intentionality was painted in the Dennettian way, but it nevertheless reflects the current state of the art in the study of intentionality. Current views have evolved due to the progress in the domains of systems thinking, philosophy, evolutionary biology, and computer science. Freud presented his claims concerning the essence of the unconscious decades previously, and, considering the era, it was a rather natural choice to use the term "mental" to refer to the competencies of the unconscious. In contemporary terms, these competencies are based on as-if intentionality (or, in terms of the above "Dennettian" picture, biological intentionality).

The three-sphere view and the branching psychoanalysis of the post-Freudian times

Recent psychoanalytic writings especially are rarely explicit on whether the expression "mental unconscious" possesses a particular meaning, or if it is just a Freudian turn of phrase. It has to be also noted that several alternative conceptions for the "Freudian" unconscious have evolved: Lacanian psychoanalysis, the hermeneutic view of psychoanalysis, narrative psychoanalysis. Constructivist and postmodern views of psychoanalysis also contain implications concerning the nature of the unconscious. The psychoanalyst Owen Reinik states in *The International Journal of Psychoanalysis*,

> Increasingly, I believe, contemporary analysts (. . .) are using the term *unconscious* to denote simply that which an observer might expect to be within an individual's conscious awareness, but which is not. [1998, p. 495]

We can sketch four basic attitudes towards the existence of the unconscious: the unconscious is

(a) just the competencies, processes, predispositions, and functions of the brain;
(b) one way of talking about the brain and behaviour; a helpful or necessary theoretical concept;
(c) something—an entity, sphere, or space—that in principle can be measured and/or observed;
(d) something—an entity, sphere, or space—that is beyond our senses and methods of science.

Attitude (a) represents the cognitivists' two-sphere view, and (b) should be seen as a practical enlargement of it—if an analyst says that the Freudian view of the unconscious is a practical tool for a clinician, a cognitivist should not have anything against it. Attitudes (c) and (d) spell out the three-sphere view: "between" consciousness and the brain there is something on which we have not made (direct) observations. In fact, (c) and (d) differ in only one respect: whether or not one believes that the third sphere may be observed *in principle*. A supporter of (d) possesses a mystical or mystifying relation toward the unconscious, and thus (d) cannot be approached scientifically.

Alasdair Macintyre states,

> Either the unconscious is an inaccessible realm of inaccessible enti-
> ties existing in its own right or it is a theoretical and unobservable
> entity introduced to explain and relate a number of otherwise inex-
> plicable phenomena. If it is the first, then being a real existent it
> requires evidence for its existence to be credible. [2004, pp. 96–97]

Macintyre talks here about (c) and (b), and we must ask what might
be counted as evidence in favour of (c).

As noted above, mental terms are currently used in order to
refer to subjective feelings and mental images appearing in one's
consciousness, and in that case the reference point is evident for
everybody (excluding, of course, some philosophers). When the
suggested mental thing is "the unconscious", however, feelings and
images cannot serve as determinants—characteristic of feelings and
mental images are their phenomenal qualities, which appear in the
domain of consciousness. Thus, mental unconscious and (c) appear
as a logical impossibility, an oxymoron.

It has to be also asked what the supposed third sphere of the
three-sphere view is like, where and how would it exist, and how
would unconscious desires and fears exist in the scope of it.
Reasonable answers to these questions cannot even be conceived—
conceiving the third sphere appears more difficult than conceiving
a fourth dimension of space. Here, one cannot avoid thinking that
there is similarity between Descartes' view on the soul and the
psychoanalytic idea on the third sphere: both presume a mystical
sphere or an entity that cannot be taken as the object of scientific
study. Benjamin Rubinstein (1997, pp. 49–55) is perhaps the only
psychoanalyst who has, in a plain and explicit manner, stated the
core problem with the third sphere: supposing that there are unconscious mental entities that do not become reduced to neurophysiological matters implies dualism. The psychoanalytic ideas around
the unconscious form a specific branch of dualism, which might be
named *psychoanalytic dualism*.

The mental unconscious and other unobservables

Psychoanalysts hasten to remind us that the talk about unobservable matters is not restricted to the realm of psychoanalysis—non-

observable electrons are a core element of present-day physicists' world-view, for example. Thus, why should psychoanalysts cast off the concept of the mental unconscious?

It is clear that one cannot just arbitrarily postulate non-observable entities—there have to be grounds for that. There are precise reasons (based on empirical observations and inference) for supposing the existence of non-observable electrons. We cannot study those reasons here, but it is the case that physicists have a consensus on the existence of electrons. In contrast, among behavioural scientists there is no consensus on the existence of the third sphere and the mental unconscious.

Psychoanalysts often state that the psychoanalytic setting is a laboratory providing data that is not accessible for other behavioural scientists, and that the data should be taken as evidence of the mental unconscious. Lavinia Gomez claims that the third sphere "... has no language of its own. It cannot be broken down into mental and physical components, yet it can only be thought of as though it were mental, or as though it were physical" (Gomez, 2005, pp. 9–10).

This kind of thinking might be called metaphysics, or natural philosophy, and it even contains cosmological aspects. Gomez's view is very distant from the clinical data, which is about human interaction and verbalizations of the stream of consciousness—psychoanalysts shake hands with their analysands, see them lying on the couch, and hear them talking, crying, and laughing. The psychoanalytic setting is really a kind of laboratory, but psychoanalysts' observations are not *fundamentally* different from those of other behavioural scientists—psychoanalytic technique cannot be equated with microscopes, telescopes, and brain-scanning techniques. Thus, observations concerning analysands' (mainly verbal) behaviour do not legitimate the *ontological* (or metaphysical) presupposition on the existence of the sphere containing unobservable matters. In order not to cast off the presupposition of the third sphere too hastily, let us take a look at another unobservable, which was debated in Freud's times.

At the end of the twentieth century, physicists shared the ontological presupposition that the ether fills the otherwise empty parts of the universe. X-rays, for example, are comprised of longitudinal vibrations of it. In 1902, Henri Poincaré claimed that the ether was

at most an abstract frame of reference that could not be given physical properties. When Albert Einstein published his theory of relativity three years later, the majority of physicists then thought the
presupposition of ether was useless. After that, serious talk about
ether among physicists was restricted to the Teutonic and Soviet
science domains in the 1930s (Kragh, 1999).

In his article on the unobservables in scientific theories, Bonioli
states,

> Usually, these unobservables serve the purpose of supporting some
> internal consistence [of a theory], but their introduction creates the
> suspicion that the theorisation might be replaced by another one
> which, besides representing the same aspects represented by the
> first, does not involve the introduction of unobservables. [2000,
> p. 187]

Bonioli's statement reflects the relation between ether theories and
Einstein's relativity theory. We must ask whether it also reflects the
situation between the Freudian three-sphere view and the two-
sphere view (and the four-level model introduced in Chapter Five):
the latter seems to make the presupposition concerning the mental
unconscious useless. According to the principle known as Occam's
razor, the simpler model should be favoured.

Prior to the theory of relativity there were certain plausible
reasons to "believe in" the ether. Similarly, in Freud's time, the
foundations of the two-sphere view were not as solid as currently,
and there were reasons to presuppose the third sphere. We should,
however, question the present-day reasons. Progress in the scope of
both theory and empirical research led physicists to abandon the
idea of ether, and we should ask that, if the matters presented so far
in this chapter do not give a reason to abandon the three-sphere
view, which theoretical and empirical findings would? To put it in
the Popperian way: which finding would falsify the presupposition
of the mental unconscious?

All in all, it is difficult to see, first, how psychoanalysts' data
might support metaphysical speculations like those of Gomez's,
and why the practical affair of psychotherapy should be anchored
to such speculations. Second, it has to be said that the connection
between physicists' inferring unobservable electrons on the one

hand, and psychoanalysts' inferring the unobservable mental unconscious on the other, is very loose.

Thus, when depending on the ordinary sense of mental concepts, it is difficult to present arguments in favour of the existence of the unconscious that are something "more" than (b) presupposes (see p. 55). As presented in Chapter Two, there are many mental terms, and they have possessed variety of meanings. One is not restricted to the ordinary sense of mental concepts, and "mental" may be defined in a way that renders possible the talk about the mental unconscious. As a matter of fact, Kukla and Walmsley (2006, pp. 41–42) have claimed that, when introducing the idea of the mental unconscious, Freud actually proposed that we changed the definitions of mentalistic terms.

We must ask, however, what would be won if the term "mental" were given an extraordinary meaning. Such conceptual acrobatics would make no difference to the factual essence of the unconscious, and it creates unnecessary obstacles for interdisciplinary collaboration. Giving the "mind" a definition that is not anchored to the phenomenal qualities may also lead to absurdities—it may turn out that mechanisms like cars containing in-car computers, for example, possess mental unconscious, although not having phenomenal consciousness.

It is difficult to avoid thinking that in psychoanalytic circles it is considered necessary to try to save the cornerstone set by Freud at all costs. Views like Gomez's natural philosophy appear as sublimated (or disguised) psychoanalytic dualism.

*   *   *

Development of the methods of neuroscience provided grounds for the two-sphere view, but it also led to a revival of neurophysiology (and Freud's *Project*) in the domain of psychoanalysis, and that way led to the emergence of the endeavour of neuropsychoanalysis. There is a certain fascination towards neuropsychoanalysis in academic circles, and neuropsychoanalysis also enables newspapers and magazines to write popular "Revival of Freud" articles. Because neuropsychoanalysis is an interdisciplinary endeavour sharing much common ground with cognitive neuroscience, it is very interesting to see whether it leans towards the two-sphere or the three-sphere view. I focus on this issue below.

Neuropsychoanalysis and the unconscious

Among psychoanalysts and psychoanalytically orientated researchers there has, of course, always been interest in empirical and neurophysiological issues (for a review, see Levin, 1998). Nevertheless, such an interest has played a minor role in the realm of psychoanalysis—an average analyst of the twentieth century did not care whether or not psychoanalytic claims were supported or contradicted by empirical research, or how psychoanalytic concepts such as censorship and repressed contents would appear from the perspective of neuroscience.

Anyway, in 1999 the first volume of the journal *Neuro-Psychoanalysis* was published. Neuropsychoanalysis aims to find neural counterparts for psychoanalytic concepts, and to shed light on the neural basis for the phenomena found in psychoanalytic practice. The journal promotes a genuine interdisciplinary spirit: its editorial advisory board contains leading neuroscientists, and it has published articles and commentaries by such distinguished non-psychoanalytic scientists as Jaak Panksepp, Francis Crick, Benjamin Libet, and Ray Jackendoff. Neuropsychoanalysis is focused on Freudian thinking—names such as Klein, Jung, and Lacan rarely appear in the journal—and there is a relatively strong emphasis on metapsychology, especially in the writings of Mark Solms, who can be said to be the founder (or the "father") of neuropsychoanalysis, and who is one of the editors of *Neuro-Psychoanalysis*.

The aims and basis of neuropsychoanalysis seem to fit well with present-day cognitivists' views, and at the same time it is without doubt preferably a psychoanalysts' affair. We might suppose that through the subject unconscious it would be revealed whether neuropsychoanalysis is psychoanalytic or neuroscientific at heart: in the case that it tends towards the three-sphere view, there is considerable tension between it and cognitive neuroscience and neuro-psychiatry. The two-sphere view as cornerstone would mean a rebellious position in the psychoanalytic community. Let us begin with the subject by studying Mark Solms' stand.

In his target article for *The Journal of the American Psychoanalytic Association*, Solms (1997) explicitly rejects the "truism" that conscious experiences are caused by brain processes (i.e., the two-sphere view): "It is, I believe a statement to which no psychoanalyst should ever assent, as it flatly contradicts the fundamental assumption on which the whole of our discipline rests" (*ibid.*, p. 681). Solms bases his view on Freud's conception (or metaphor) of the nature of consciousness: consciousness is like perception. Just as material things around us may be seen or not, mental things in our minds may be seen or they may remain hidden. According to Solms/ Freud (and also Gomez, 2005), the brain does not cause consciousness, but "rather the abstract, natural thing that generates both of them, and that can never be known directly" (Solms 1997, p. 701). There is no doubt that Solms radically contradicts the cognitive two-sphere view. The words ". . . and that can never be known directly" even hint that Solms is an advocate of the (mystifying) basic attitude (d).

Both psychoanalytic and cognitivist commentators strongly challenged Solms' view, however: the perception metaphor is erroneous, Solms has misread Freud, Solms' view reflects Kantian transcendential idealism . . . Howard Shevrin, another leading figure of the neuropsychoanalytic approach, even holds that Solms was sliding into (subjective) idealism as advocated by Bishop Berkeley at the beginning of the eighteenth century (Shevrin, 1997, pp. 746–747). How, then, does Shevrin himself approach the subject of the unconscious?

Conscious and Unconscious Processes: Psychodynamic, Cognitive, and Neurophysiological Convergences (Shevrin, Bond, Brakel, Hertel, & Williams 1996) is an interdisciplinary study on the unconscious. The authors introduce the "psychoanalytic", "cognitive", and "psychophysiological" theories of the unconscious at the beginning of the book. Then their extensive and sophisticated series of research projects using the methods of psychodynamic evaluation (three interviews), psychological testing (WAIS-R, Rorschach, TAT), and laboratory experimentation (using a tachistoscope to present rapid flashes of words related to the subjects' intrapsychic conflicts, and recording their ERPs) is introduced.

For Shevrin and his co-authors, William James and Norman Dixon (a well-known researcher on subliminal perception) are representatives of the two-sphere view. Shevrin and his colleagues argue in favour of the existence of the *psychological* unconscious quite apart from the plain neurophysiological unconscious (i.e., they advocate the three-sphere view). They base their arguments on subliminal perception (*ibid.*, pp. 264–266). In that context it has been found that flashing the word "nurse" subliminally (the subject does not know he or she has seen it), for example, leads to more rapid recognition of the word "doctor". Their reasoning is as follows:

> If only the conscious can be psychological, then nonconscious neurophysiological processes must lack "aboutness", for that is what makes something psychological. However, as we will try to show below, subliminal studies, including our own, demonstrate that "aboutness" does exist in the absence of consciousness. [*ibid.*, p. 265]

Since Brentano's studies, "aboutness" has been commonly seen as a criterion for intentionality (and mind). Shevrin and his co-authors, however, do not present the logic behind aboutness, psychological unconscious, and intentionality. They do not even mention the term "intentionality", and consequently do not study the distinction between intrinsic and as-if intentionality, for example. This shortcoming makes one wonder whether they have read even an introductory article on intentionality, or whether they suppose that the reader has not done so. Thus, their approach appears as a trick—aboutness is not a magical word that gives a being a psyche. Showing through the study of subliminal perception that neurophysiological structures possess as-if intentionality is not an argument in favour of the psychological unconscious (whatever that means).

Shevrin and his colleagues state,

> When we speak of Mr. A's *unconscious* rage, Mr. C's *unconscious* desire to submit himself homosexually, or Mr. B's *repressed* perception of his father as fatally ill, we are talking about mental contents that are represented in the mind and instantiated neurophysiologically. [*ibid.*, p. 270, original emphases]

Thus, it is clear that they advocate the three-sphere view: the mental unconscious exists apart from the brain and consciousness (". . . represented in the mind *and* instantiated neurophysiologically"). The following citations contain echoes from vitalism: ". . . it is essential to talk about a *psychological* unconscious which is embodied in still unknown neurophysiological processes but for which we have discovered certain useful markers" (ibid., p. 265). They portray the psychological unconscious and repressed mental contents as Cartesian "animal spirits" embodied in "still unknown" neurophysiological processes. It is worth mentioning that Shevrin (2004, p. 150) also holds that unconscious fantasies are one important form of subjectivity.

According to Solms (1997, p. 691), "Psychoanalysis and PET scanning . . . study one and the same underlying object: the mental apparatus and its functions", and Shulman and Rothman (2000) have disagreed with that (see also Shulman & Reiser, 2004). They claim that functional imaging methods do not directly measure mental processes (Shulman & Rothman, 2000, p. 164), and that such experiments "are designed to exclude the subjective brain activity that is the essence of the psychoanalytic field" (ibid., p. 169) Their logic is difficult to follow—what is *subjective* brain activity? In any case, it is clear that both their and Solms' conceptions differ from the two-sphere view of the cognitivists.

Yoram Yovell, one of the editors of Neuro-Psychoanalysis, holds that although "most contemporary philosophers, the majority of contemporary neuroscientists and cognitive psychologists . . . firmly reject" the idea of the unconscious level of mentation, "there are conceptual as well as experimental reasons to hypothesize that such a level exists" (Yovell, 2004, p. 156). He suggests that the human tendency for self-deception is one of the latter. However, the leading theory on self-deception (Mele, 2001) applies the two-sphere view.

Mauro Mancia's (2004) book, Feeling the Words—Neuropsychoanalytic Understanding of Memory and the Unconscious, condenses some presuppositions and lines of thought typical for neuropsychoanalysis. As usual in neuropsychoanalysis, Mancia's explicit aim is to integrate psychoanalytic views with those of neuroscience: "The possibility of identifying explicit and implicit memories with respectively the repressed and unrepressed offers exciting prospects for integration between the neurosciences and psychoanalysis, and possibly establishing some anatomo-functional correlations" (ibid., p. 47). He continues by stating

This implies one assumption: that the experiences, life events, emotions, fantasies and defences around which the person's unconscious psychic reality has been organized, from birth and throughout life, are in fact stored in the nervous structures used by implicit and explicit memory. [*ibid.*]

Should one—a neuroscientist, for example—accept that assumption? It depends on what "unconscious psychic reality" is supposed to mean. The expression seems to refer to the third sphere—the ontological presupposition not accepted by present-day neuroscience. Mancia, however, continues by citing Freud, and does not explicate the assumption. It would be fair for the reader, and useful for the integration of neurosciences and psychoanalysis, to focus on this matter. Why does Mancia—similarly to his fellow neuropsychoanalysts—not do that? Is neuropsychoanalysis interested in just superficial integration, and willing to hide its psychoanalytic dualism?

Mancia's book also contains a chapter on mental pain. He states,

> When I talk of mental pain I am referring to *unconscious psychic suffering* that leaks out into consciousness and invests one's whole being. It is human beings' companion from their earliest relations, developing in parallel as children structure their internal world and their representations, until thought takes form. For these ontogenetic reasons, therefore, mental suffering is intrinsic to humankind and therefore demands prime position in any psychoanalytic theory of the mind. [*ibid.*, p. 210; my italics]

Again, Mancia presents a very confusing presupposition ("unconscious psychic suffering"), and even holds that it is "intrinsic to humankind", and that it "demands a prime position in any psychoanalytic theory of mind". However, he does not care to tell us what he is talking about. Thus, a reader is left wondering *how on earth suffering could be unconscious*.

All in all, it seems that there is a legion of third-sphere concepts (repressed ideas, desire, fear, and even fantasy; psychological unconscious; unconscious psychic reality; unconscious suffering; censorship; mental apparatus) reflecting psychoanalytic dualism. But is psychoanalytic dualism a secret doctrine (or "code") that psychoanalytic folks know but avoid expressing in public, or is it confusing for insiders, too?

In Chapter Seven of his book, *The Rediscovery of the Mind* (Searle, 1992), the philosopher John Searle explicitly throws doubt on psychoanalytic dualism. Searle advocates the monistic view that the mind is a biological phenomenon, an aspect of the brain and its processes. As with researchers publishing in the scope of cognitivistic tradition in general, he represents the two-sphere view. Searle's contribution has given rise to some discussion that sheds light on the above question.

Searle states, "But he [Freud] has not made intelligible what events could be going on in the brain in addition to the neurophysiological events . . ." (*ibid.*, p. 168). He also says that the idea that there might be unconscious mental intentional phenomena that are in principle inaccessible to consciousness "violates a logical constraint on the notion of intentionality", and that Freud's view is hard to interpret otherwise than "implying dualism". However, Searle does not see a fundamental error in Freud's thinking: the difference between his (two-sphere) view and that of Freud's (three-sphere view) is just terminological.

Let us note that Searle's view is anything but new. In his book *Psychotherapy*, from the year 1909, Freud's contemporary Hugo Münsterberg argued in favour of a view that is identical with that of Searle's (Münsterberg, 1909, pp. 125–157). Regrettably, Freud did not answer Münsterberg's arguments in "The unconscious", which came out six years later—he just talked about "The stubborn denial of a psychical character to latent mental acts . . ." (Freud, 1915e).

Several psychoanalytic authors have responded to Searle's critique—in a very critical manner (Gillett, 1996; Palombo, 1994; Shevrin, 1990; Smith, 1999, pp. 137–155). In our article "On the nature of repressed contents—a working through of John Searle's critique" (Talvitie & Ihanus, 2003), which appeared in *Neuro-psychoanalysis*, Juhani Ihanus and I made a diplomatic effort. We argued that the psychoanalytic community should accept Searle's two-sphere view (and also applied, rather clumsily, the computer metaphor).

The commentators on our target article, all distinguished scholars in the field, disagreed with us: the question concerning the mental essence of the unconscious is not just a terminological one—*the unconscious really is mental*. According to Joel Weinberger, "A cognitive scientist and/or social psychologist would be perfectly comfortable with it [our conception of the unconscious] . . ." (Weinberger, 2003, p. 152). However, he held that our article contained "conceptual and terminological confusions", and that we did not, in fact, deal with repression. Thus, he could not "feel comfortable in offering a sensible critique" of our article.

We leaned on Searle's book, and thus it should be no surprise that the other two commentators—Linda Brakel and David Livingstone Smith—took Searle and his philosophy as the main target of their critique. Our response, "What is it like to be unconsciously mental?" (paraphrasing Thomas Nagel's [1974] classic article "What is it like to be a bat?"), was arguably a more significant contribution than the article itself. For one thing, we focused more strongly on the supposed mental essence of the unconscious, and for another we tried to avoid philosophical discussion and insisted on concrete evidence of the existence of mental unconscious states—the commentators did not give any.

Brakel (2003, p. 143) stated in her commentary: "For something to qualify as a mental state . . . it would need to be first-personal, subjective and intrinsically intentional". Later, she added "meaning" and "representational" to the list. In our response we argued that, apart from the "representational", neural states cannot be described through such attributes.

Smith (2003a; see also Smith 2003b, pp. 92–95) took from Freud's writings the so-called "continuity argument", which gave the (main) reason why Freud held the unconscious to be mental. This argument could be briefly summarized as follows. Human consciousness contains "gaps"—sometimes we "sleep on" a problem and wake up with an answer, or a solution to a problem suddenly pops up in our mind. This means that we have unconsciously processed an idea. Plain neurophysiological matters cannot produce such a competence, and thus unconscious processing must possess the property of "mental". We might say that, for Smith, an unconscious lacking mental properties is not "intelligent enough" to produce the phenomena psychoanalysts and other people have noticed. Our response was in accordance with the Aristotelian and Leibnizean spirit of the cognitive orientation: if a mechanical (or digital) computer can carry out a complicated task, we have no reason to suppose that the non-mental brain could not do so.

It is worth noting here that Smith did not explain what the mental essence of the unconscious was like, or how it would make the brain more intelligent. He might have argued that, as a matter of fact, the problem was with flexibility: computer intelligence is still quite restricted (context dependent), whereas human information processing is characterized by flexibility. However, the same problem holds as with intelligence: the presupposition that the unconscious is mental cannot be a solution to any problem unless one is able to tell what the "mentalness" of the brain is, and how that increases intelligence or flexibility.

The philosopher Thomas Natsoulas was asked to comment on our article, but his commentary was not available for Volume 5, Issue 2, 2003. Perhaps he became interested in our ideas only after he had read the discussion between us and the reviewers—his commentary (Natsoulas, 2004) appeared in Issue 1 of Volume 6, and was considerably longer than our original article.

Natsoulas also saw the unconscious as mental, and he treated the subject in terms of philosophy. His writing offered no evidence of the mental essence of the unconscious either, which we insisted on in our response to the other commentators. Instead, he gave us labels and advice: "I sense in them [VT&JI] a return of behaviorism in a new guise" (Natsoulas 2004, p. 105);

> I would guess that Talvitie and Ihanus subscribe broadly to an eliminativist philosophy of science . . . They need to adopt and develop a more critical attitude toward their own statements. Using a neater or more scientist vocabulary than others is not enough. The attractiveness that their approach holds for key neurophysiological and philosophical personnel in our universities does not suffice either. [*ibid.*, p. 106]

Thus, Natsoulas agreed with Weinberger in that our ideas worked outside psychoanalysis but not within its scope. His long commentary gives rise to an impression that we had touched on an important question. However, it did not shed light on why we perhaps ought to consider the unconscious as being mental.

* * *

The above considerations were about the grounds on which some researchers close to neuropsychoanalysis advocate Freud's idea that the unconscious is mental. The following four conclusions can be drawn from the above study.

1. Leading neuropsychoanalysts lean on Freud's three-sphere view on the mind/brain (the brain—mental unconscious—consciousness), and thus reject the two-sphere view of the cognitive orientation (the brain—consciousness).
2. There is serious disagreement among neuropsychoanalysts concerning the grounds on which the idea of the unconscious as being mental could be advocated.
3. The presupposition of the mental unconscious is not only lacking evidence, but it is not even conceivable where the third sphere would exist, what it would be like, and how desires, fantasies, and ideas might exist in the domain of it.
4. Neuropsychoanalysis has been rather reluctant to place its commitment to psychoanalytic dualism under scrutiny.

Thus, it is an understatement to claim that there are good reasons to abandon the three-sphere view—it is a serious obstacle for frank and fruitful collaboration with cognitive neuroscience and neuropsychiatry. For the sake of the future and scientific status of psychoanalysis, it would be rational to adopt the two-sphere view, and it is difficult to see why (even neuro-) psychoanalysts get stuck in psychoanalytic dualism. Why is the three-sphere view so important for some psychoanalysts? How is it possible that, at the same time, some analysts are very liberal, using the term unconscious "to denote simply that which an observer might expect to be within an individual's conscious awareness, but which is not" (Reinik, 1998, p. 495)? Overall, why do practising psychoanalysts care at all about issues falling in the domain of philosophy of the mind? One cannot resist thinking that the three-sphere view is an issue of faith—it is widely "believed in" among psychoanalytic folk.

Brakel (2003, p. 146) closed her commentary with the remark that adopting Searle's view "threatens to separate the practice of clinical psychoanalysis from its foundational theory. Such a separation would strike a serious blow both to practice and to theory . . ." Behind Natsoulas's arrogance there seems to be a serious worry as well. It seems that the issues around the three-sphere view cannot be approached by depending on just rational argumentation. Thus, let us briefly examine two perspectives on them—one sociological, and another concerning the tools of a practising psychoanalyst.

On the sociology of the Freudian unconscious

Perhaps more than any other post-Galilean theory, Freud's views have given rise to, say, ideological reactions among both his followers and his critics. In the psychoanalytic community, in the beginning, conflicts took place between Freud and some of his close collaborators. Subsequently there have been convergences between Freudians, neo-Freudians, and non-Freudians, and, in addition to that, also disputes on who really represents Freud's legacy. In general, psychoanalytic schools of post-Freudian times have had a tendency to be driven to inner conflicts—let us just mention the controversy between (M.) Kleinians and (A.) Freudians in the UK, and the dramas between several schools founded by Jacques Lacan in France.

For many, both followers and enemies, Freud's ideas and theories are something wholly different from just hypotheses, or a scientist's models created a century ago. In many former and also current psychoanalytic communities, disagreeing with Freud has not been seen as a factual issue, but a psychological tendency that can and should be understood in terms of psychoanalytic theory. In psychoanalysis, the unconscious is anything but a peripheral issue, and there has been considerable social pressure to accept Freud's view as it stands. If a psychoanalytic candidate asks in a meeting how the unconscious actually exists, the emperor's new clothes effect most probably does not come up. Quite the contrary— the candidate is advised to study his resistance toward psychoanalysis. For those who are not familiar with this (dark) side of social life in psychoanalytic communities, let us present two examples.

Benjamin Rubinstein, a Finnish-born psychoanalyst, was trained in the Menninger clinic in Topeka in the middle of the twentieth century. In his final examination, Rubinstein criticized Freud's sexual theory, which led to notable controversies. Rubinstein was recommended to further analysis, and his psychoanalyst and teacher Karl Menninger wrote in a letter that ". . . you [Rubinstein] are handicapped in your vision by some unanalyzed factors" (Rubinstein, 1997, p. 621). Later, Menninger also tried to prevent Rubinstein from getting a licence from the American Psychoanalytic Association.

At the beginning of his career, the Nobel laureate Eric Kandel considered becoming a psychoanalyst. In 1965, Kandel told his friend's father, a respected psychoanalyst, that he had changed his plans and was going to become a researcher in the domain of neuroscience. The psychoanalyst looked at Kandel "in amazement" and muttered: "It sounds to me that as if your analysis was not fully successful; you seem never really to have quite resolved your transference" (Kandel, 2005, p. xx).

When it comes to the significance of Freud's view on the unconscious for a practising psychoanalyst, one must not underestimate the fact that it has laid logical grounds for his or her interventions. The aim of psychoanalysis is to try to relieve an analysand's disorders by making the repressed conscious. This aim has been traditionally worked out by thinking of the (mental) unconscious as a place, sphere, or space where repressed ideas lie, and from which they may be brought into the domain of consciousness. If the three-sphere view is abandoned in favour of the two-sphere view, this logic collapses.

The curative power of psychoanalytic treatment does not, however, lie in the analyst's "faith" in the mental unconscious, or commitment to the three-sphere view. To put it in other words, as far as the psychoanalytic technique has shown itself to be successful, it cannot become ruined if an analyst adopts the two-sphere view. The shift from the three-sphere view to the two-sphere view means just that an analyst reflected which concepts are clinician's tools, metaphors, and which refer to actual neural and mental structures and mechanisms. Thus, there is no reason for the worries that Brakel (and Natsoulas) presented.

In the following chapters, certain foundational elements of psychoanalysis are re-thought, and how we should approach repression and becoming conscious of the repressed in terms of the two-sphere view is sketched.

CHAPTER FOUR

On the competencies of the neural unconscious

The preceding chapters have circulated between three entangled topics: *phenomena* that have been thought to be caused by unconscious matters; the *essence of the unconscious*; and how those phenomena could and should be *explained*. Below, the circulation will continue, although this chapter also has a specific subject: it begins with the study of how psychoanalytic notions could be presented in terms of the two-sphere view.

When such a challenge is faced, the first thing that comes to mind is that perhaps the (psychoanalysts') "mental unconscious" could be simply replaced by (cognitivists') "neural unconscious". This general idea can be divided into more specific ones: the intrinsic intentionality of the mental unconscious might be replaced by the as-if intentionality of the neural unconscious, and instead of thinking that repressed ideas were stored in the unconscious mind, it might be thought that they are stored by the brain.

This line of thought implies that this chapter is focused on the competencies of the neural unconscious. Intentionality is a philosophical term, which is intimately connected to the psychological terms "representation", "desire", "motive", "wish", and "goal-directed behaviour". Thus, it is not a surprise that the competencies are studied through them.

Representing and detecting

The above idea that repressed contents are just neural representations whose activation is inhibited is easy to figure out by thinking of a computer. A computer contains digital representations of, among other things, the pictures one has taken with one's digital camera. By clicking an appropriate icon, the digital representation of a certain picture becomes activated. Paraphrasing Freudian thinking, we might say that by clicking the icon the picture is brought or transformed from the hardware of the computer (the brain, the unconscious) into the scope of the screen (consciousness). We can think that the representation can also be prevented from being brought into the domain of the screen/consciousness.

But do present-day views actually support the idea that repressed ideas might be represented by the brain in a similar way to that in which pictures are represented by the hardware of a computer? It is least difficult to approach this question in the case of repressed *memories*. Laymen (and, some decades ago, also researchers) used to think of remembering in terms of a store, from which memories—or representations of past events—are brought into the scope of consciousness. Present-day views of psychology, however, strongly contradict this kind of thinking.

We must think that the brain does contain memory traces of some kind. Those traces are, however, in contrast to a computer's representations, fragmentary and unsophisticated. Behind the experience of remembering a certain event there are much more complicated matters than just activation of a single memory trace or representation. There is a dynamic process that is participated in by memory cues, logical reasoning, one's feelings towards the event, and one's hopes and fears concerning what was the actual state of things.

One may fail to remember an event, but, in addition to that, one's "memory performance" is always more or less imperfect, biased, and distorted. Memory and remembering has been studied more than any other psychological issue, and currently there is a consensus that recollections are not just retrieved from memory, but that remembering should be seen as *construction* above all—an experience of remembering a certain event is an end-point of a dynamic process (see, for example, Edelman & Tononi, 2000, pp. 93–101; Schacter, 1996).

Thus, it seems that in the case of repressed memories we cannot amend the three-sphere view by just thinking that repressed ideas are actually neural representations that are prevented from becoming activated. Instead, we should think that when a certain memory does not come into mind, one or several (neural and conscious) processes have been inhibited. This idea is elaborated in the next chapter. Let us now take a brief look at how the brain is thought to represent things.

According to present-day views (see, for example Churchland, 1996; Spivey, 2006), the brain does not represent objects as wholes, but as a bunch of features. Consider how one's mother's face is represented by the brain. Each face is a unique composition of a certain kind of nose, mouth, colour of, and distance between, the eyes, silhouette, and so on. For the brain, mother's face is simply a composition of such features. Each feature is detected by a certain neuron (or neural network); the neuron fires when the feature appears. The activity (firing rate) of neurons also varies. A neuron detecting a certain kind of nose, for example, fires in a high frequency when such a nose is seen, and a nose that approximates it causes lower frequency firing. Thus, in terms of neurophysiology, recognizing mother's face means that the neuron A (detecting the form of nose) fires in a frequency of X , the neuron B (mouth) fires in a frequency of Y, and the neuron J (distance between the eyes) fires in a frequency of Z. The neural representation of mother's face is a profile: how neurons specializing in face recognition react to mother's face. The profile is also called a *population code*.

We are able to recognize faces even in unusual conditions—when seeing only part of it very rapidly in the dark, or a caricature of a familiar face. Thus, in order to recognize an object, a sensation does not need to match completely with the neural representation. As a matter of fact, sensations never match completely with the representation. In his book *The Continuity of Mind*, Michael Spivey (2006) spells out the interesting consequences of this fact.

Recognizing an object is not an either/or issue. Let us think that the number one reflects the (theoretical) situation that a perception completely matches with neural representation. When we recognize an object consciously ("hey, that's my mother"), the match is, say, somewhere between 0.8 and 1.0. However, when we see somebody in the dark, for example, there may be 0.8. match with the neural representation of mother, 0.6 match with aunt, and 0.5 match with a neighbour. Thus, from the perspective of the brain, a perceived object is *several persons at the same time.*

In the case of panic attacks, for example, a stimulus related to a traumatic situation is not necessarily consciously recognized, but nevertheless triggers an attack. Thus, the brain is also able to detect stimuli.

Spivey emphasizes that our talk about mental states is very inexact. In terms of neurophysiology, each mental state—recognizing one's mother, wanting to lose weight, hating one's sister, or believing that sport is good for one, for example—corresponds with a certain population code. In practice it is, of course, impossible to identify the population code, since there are 100 billion neurons in the brain. In any case, one mental term actually refers to several kinds of mental states: one may say, for example, that one hates one's sister, taxes, country music, and headaches. It must be also noted that hating one's sister today because she joined a racist political party is quite different from hating her next moth because of her behaving badly when drunk. Because a single mental term covers several different mental states, it also has several corresponding population codes of neurons. Thus, in our speech there is just one "hate", but it stands for many phenomenal and neural states.

All in all, our everyday talk about hates and wishes simplifies the actual state of things a great deal. Spivey states that we, or our brains, are good at *discriminating* things: when we get robbed, we are often able to tell whether or not the person we meet later is the robber. What we are bad at is *describing our mental states verbally*: the robber will be caught based on our verbal description only if he or she has a special characteristic like a scar.

Unconscious neural algorithms

In Chapter Two we studied empirical research of the cognitive unconscious (implicit knowledge). Let us remind ourselves of the basic procedure of this. First, subjects are presented with a stimulus, or they perform a task. The second phase is conducted to show that they did not (consciously) perceive the stimulus, or that they did not notice or remember a certain aspect of the task. In the third phase they perform a task in which the stimuli presented in the first phase are helpful. If the presenting of the stimuli in the first phase (of which the subjects remained unconscious) improves the performance in the third phase, it is an indication that, first, unconscious detection occurred, and second, that unconscious memory/learning/knowledge affected performance.

As mentioned, that paradigm of research has been used in the domain of psychoanalysis, too (Pötzl's studies [1917], study of Subliminal Psychodynamic Activation). However, that paradigm focused on the competencies of the unconscious in a rather artificial manner: studies based on octagons and how flashing the word "nurse" affects recognition of the word "doctor" do not shed much light on how unconscious matters affect our daily life. Anyway, we do not detect stimuli unconsciously just in the laboratory, but our practices are based on unconsciously driven processes.

When learning to drive a car, for example, we think all the time about such things as changing gear, braking, and keeping on the road. Gradually, those matters become automatic, and later such ideas do not appear in the scope of consciousness while driving. One may even be totally unaware later of what happened on a familiar journey from home to work. Thus, a goal or an aim that once was conscious still directs behaviour. Similarly, a pianist playing Rachmaninoff's fifth piano concerto in public does not think of which key to press next, although having done so thousands of times when practising the concerto.

Several researchers—let us just mention Jerry Fodor (1983, modularity of mind), Bernard Baars (1997, global workspace model), Joseph LeDoux (1998, fear conditioning) and Gerald Edelman (Edelman & Tononi, 2000; unconscious neural routines)—have sketched a rather congruent picture of those everyday notions and empirical findings: neural processes taking place in certain regions of the brain give rise to conscious states, and some other processes do not. Former (conscious) processes are flexible and rather slow, occurring in a linear way. The latter (unconscious) processes are fast, process information in a more restricted, mechanical manner, and occur in parallel.

Specific neural algorithms are formed either via evolutionary process, or in the course of personal life history, and they are triggered by certain stimuli. LeDoux (1998, p. 127) calls the stimuli triggering evolutionary based (unconscious) neural routines (or algorithms) "natural triggers". Personal routines that emerge during one's life-history are "learned triggers". Detection of the stimuli is the "appraisal mechanism". We know quite a lot about the neural basis of these mechanisms and processes (see, for example LeDoux, 1998; Squire & Kandel, 1999, pp. 157–193), but that is not crucial for us here. The important thing is that we have both empirical evidence and neurophysiological models of how unconscious processes direct our behaviour. Let us note that the term "unconscious" in front of "neural algorithm" is, strictly speaking, unnecessary, since all neural processes are unconscious; it is just that some of them give rise to conscious states.

Nowadays, it is commonplace to refer to conscious processes by terms such as "explicit knowledge" and "declarative memory", and unconscious ones by "implicit memory", "procedural memory", and "tacit knowledge". Neuropsychoanalytic writings, too, often introduce neurophysiological details of explicit and implicit aspects of processing. The rather general perspective of these two aspects of processing leads to sometimes confusing presuppositions. Mancia (2004, p. 32), for example, suggests that a child's fantasies and defences from the pre-verbal and pre-symbolic stages are stored in the implicit memory. It is, however, far from clear how a conscious state (a fantasy) and a behavioural disposition (a defence) were stored in implicit memory, and how they might later affect one's behaviour. Implicit memories cannot be made conscious, and thus implicit knowledge/memory cannot be equated with the repressed or the mental unconscious (Talvitie & Ihanus, 2002).

In order to make the picture more simple, and that way also more revealing, it is reasonable to present the distinction implicit/ explicit knowledge in terms of two components: *detections* and *neural algorithms*. When there is a sensation, an object is either detected or not, and when it is detected, it affects one's behaviour only when triggering neural processes. A conscious detection means that one has a sensation of hearing or seeing something. A sensation either rapidly clears off, or it is attended, perhaps thought for a moment, and maybe that matter also becomes associated with another matter.

An unconscious detection does not give rise to a sensation, and as such it does not affect one's behaviour. However, if an unconscious detection triggers neural algorithms—that Edelman calls unconscious neural loops—it may have many kinds of consequences. On a more general level, unconscious neural loops are specific *information processing modes*. On a behavioural and phenomenal level, this means that, due to the unconscious detections and neural algorithms, we are liable to interpret matters in a certain way—for example paranoically, emotionally, or rationally. When unconsciously detecting a sign of danger, we behave and interpret matter in a fight-or-flight spirit, without realizing the reason for that; when detecting an erotic sign we become sexually aroused, and so on.

From the psychoanalytic perspective, this picture is very interesting. First, defence mechanisms should also be seen as unconsciously triggered information processing modes. Second, the above matters give us the neural basis of transference. In therapy sessions, when the analyst's tone of voice, manner of speech, or specific expression is common for the analysand from other relationships, the brain may detect that without conscious recognition. In the analytic setting, participants are in a non-symmetrical relation to each other: just one can see the other, and there is just one who is supposed to say what comes into his or her mind. The arrangement resembles the relation between a parent and a child, and we may suppose that the brain is able to detect that, too. In both cases the brain recognizes the match between the current and a previous interaction without conscious processing, and then triggers certain unconscious neural algorithms. Those algorithms generate behaviour and reactions that originate from the interaction with the other person.

Unconscious detection and the neural algorithms approach can be applied to psychic traumas also. Let us suppose that one evening Tom is violently robbed of his wallet in front of a record shop. The episode never comes spontaneously into his mind, although he remembers it if asked, and in that case Tom talks about the episode in a very unemotional and succinct manner. After the robbery Tom began to avoid going for walks, especially at night, because it made his hands tremble and gave rise to anxiousness. He also began to get panic attacks in situations that, at first sight, did not seem to be related to the robbery.

At the beginning of this chapter it was mentioned that, on the one hand, our brain contains memory traces of previous events, and that, on the other hand, remembering is not just activation of those traces: memory cues and reasoning are important parts of the process of remembering. Tom's behaviour may be seen in terms of this perspective as follows: After the robbery Tom quickly noticed that matters like the words "wallet", "street", and "record", and night-time in general, made him think of robbery, and made him very anxious, too. Very soon, however, the robbery vanished almost completely from his consciousness. Tom's brain learnt to detect "wallets" and "records" as signs of danger. They became, say, "reversed memory cues" that turned his attention automatically, without conscious decision, to other things and inhibited emotional processes. As a side effect, unconscious neural algorithms also caused the panic attacks.

On unconscious goals and desires

Essentially, desires and fears are similar matters. In order to be less cryptic, let us remind ourselves that they both appear as some kind of force that draws us in opposite directions—fears can be seen as "negative goals". Below, I focus on desires, but for the most part, the studies may be applied to fears, too.

The topic is complicated conceptually as well as otherwise. The term "desire" is surrounded by a swarm of interrelated and over-lapping psychological concepts: wish, motive, the purpose, goal, aim, "telos", and function of behaviour. In order to make sense of the (Freudian) idea of repressed desires, we should first get to the bottom of what the entity is like that is supposed to be repressed. However, when reading articles and books on this topic, or even after consulting dictionaries of psychology, it is difficult to identify which matters the above terms actually pinpoint.

The *Oxford Dictionary of Psychology* (Colman, 2001) and *The Penguin Dictionary of Psychology* (Reber, 1985) do not contain the entry "desire", and only from the latter can one be found for "wish": "Generally, any longing or desire" (Reber, 1985, p. 831).

Those terms are also missing from Rycroft's (1968) *A Critical Dictionary of Psychoanalysis*. This might lead us to think that the meanings of the terms are self-evident. Laplanche and Pontalis's entry "Wish (Desire)" hints that the case is actually the contrary: "Any general theory of man is bound to contain ideas too fundamental to be circumscribed; this is no doubt true of desire in the Freudian doctrine" (Laplanche & Pontalis, 1973, p. 482). Let us begin our study with these terms for motivation.

Desires, motives, and motivation

The psychoanalyst Benjamin Rubinstein's view on the essence of wish is illuminating in the case of motivation, too. He states,

> Having a wish, obviously, is not comparable to having a leg or to having an automobile. Having a wish is not having a thing, whether permanently or temporarily. As the expression is commonly used, having a wish seems to be more closely comparable to having a sense of humor than to either of the situations just mentioned. [Rubinstein, 1997, p. 542]

Rubinstein (*ibid.*, pp. 541–549) studies the essence of the term "wish" through the sentence "He has a wish to go to Italy", stating that it has two meanings.

First, such a sentence may refer to an *episode of wishing*: When one asks "Why did Tom go to a travel agency?", it is appropriate to say "Because he has a wish to go to Italy", if Tom has talked about such a wish. Thus, "wish" refers to a conscious state of the subject.

Second, the sentence may refer to *disposition to engage in activities* that may lead to going to Italy. Thus, if the sentence "Tom has a wish to go to Italy" is true, Tom will in the future do such things as checking up on how much it costs to fly to Italy. Probably he will also study what the weather is like in Italy, watch television programmes about Italy, fantasize about Italian women, and so on. Let us put the dispositional aspect another way. When there is a wish to go to Italy, many different stimuli—weather reports, eating, choosing clothes, watching football—may give rise to, or "trigger" activities and conscious states that are related to Italy. If there is no wish to go to Italy, these activities would be lacking.

Let us note that these two meanings are independent of each other: on the one hand there may be episodes of wishing that do not later affect one's behaviour, and on the other hand it is possible to possess a disposition to engage in certain activities without the conscious idea of engaging in them. The latter possibility sounds like an unconscious desire, and reminds us of the unconscious detections and neural algorithms studied above.

In psychoanalytic circles, approaches of the kind that Rubinstein advocates are often labelled as "behaviouristic" or "positivist". Such claims may be seen as reflecting the tension between the two-sphere and the three-sphere views. In any case, Rubinstein's approach fits quite well with contemporary views on motivation.

Books on motivation tell us that at the core of the branch of study in question there is the why-question concerning behaviour ("why X does Y"). More specifically, Laming (2004, p. 2) states, "For this book, motivation means the switching on of some pattern of behavior, of a program of action specified within the individual. That program might be innate or it might have been modified by experience". Weiner (1992, pp. 2–4) says that laypersons usually answer why-questions by referring to traits, stable characteristics of the person. However, he stresses that psychologists should take into account many interacting determinants of an action: traits, states, moods, emotions, conscious thoughts, unconscious attitudes, and so on.

Thus, pinpointing motives seems to be a rather peripheral issue for the study of motivation. Instead, Weiner focuses on better and worse *motivational explanations*, and states,

> . . . the goal of motivational psychology is to develop a language, an explanatory system, a conceptual representation, or what is commonly termed a *theory*, that is applicable across many domains of behavior . . . This is how the reader should think about the problem of motivation. [Weiner, 1992, p. 4]

In the case that one repeatedly thinks "I want to go to Italy", it is natural to say that the person in question has a certain wish or desire, and that the motive behind studying Italy or robbing a bank is a desire to travel to Italy. Otherwise, the idea that a desire, a wish, or a motive is a (mental) "thing" inside a person belongs to detective stories and courts of justice, not in the realm of scientific explanations. Lynne Rudder Baker's view on beliefs holds with desires and fears, too: ". . . belief is not an entity. The root idea of belief is of believing. Believing that snow is white is a property; the term 'belief' is just a nominalization of 'believing'"(Baker, 2003, p. 185). These considerations both pinpoint the problems with the expression "repressed desire", and lay ground for the logic of the four-level model introduced in the following chapter.

In the empirical research of the unconscious, the focus is on the features of stimuli: "let's show them stimuli A subliminally and see how that affects their later behaviour". Psychoanalysis, and also evolutionary psychology, approaches the unconscious from the opposite direction: how humans' "pre-wired" instincts, neural algorithms, personal and species-specific characteristics and tendencies affect how we perceive the world and ourselves. In terms of Freudian thinking, instincts cause somatic pressure that becomes reflected in the scope of the consciousness—instincts make us form ideas about how they might be satisfied. However, ideas on the objects of sexual desire and ways of satisfying this might be repressed.

Precise desires emerge in the meeting point of physiological instincts or needs on the one hand, and environment on the other. General needs concerning sex and food are . . . yes, general—as themselves they do not specify the matters that may satisfy the need or instinct. A precise desire—to make love with Alice, or to take a bottle of beer from the fridge, for example—emerges when one detects from the environment an object (or such becomes activated in the domain of consciousness) that might, based on previous experiences, satisfy the need or instinct.

Considering the problems with the Freudian three-sphere view, it may sound controversial that present views of neurosciences and empirical research might be seen as supporting some Freudian intuitions. That is, objects that have previously satisfied desires may be detected unconsciously, and detection may trigger unconscious neural loops, giving rise to (apparently) goal-directed behaviour.

Goals and goal-directed behaviour

In the scope of cognitive orientation, it is currently quite common to present that the goals of our behaviour may be unconscious. Let us take an example from Glaser and Kihlstrom's article "Compensatory automaticity: unconscious volition is not an oxymoron":

> After nearly three decades of research on automaticity and construct activation, it is increasingly clear that much of human mental life operates without awareness or intent . . . There can be nonconscious intentions (e.g., goals) that, when the potential for their imminent frustration becomes evident, automatic compensatory processes will promote and protect. [Glaser & Kihlstrom, 2005, pp. 171–172]

Thus, the study of nonconscious goals appears to be a promising meeting-point for psychoanalytic and cognitive interests.

Talk about a goal, purpose, or *telos* of a certain behaviour or act is, however, a rather confusing affair. The crucial issues are whether the goal or purpose can be shown or thought to exist somewhere or not, and whether it makes sense to talk about goals and purposes if they cannot be pinpointed. Let us look at some examples.

1. Tim decided to run a marathon next year.
2. A director sent the staff an e-mail, in which she said that the corporation aims to sell 10% more mobile telephones next year

Talk about goals and purposes is unconditionally justified when the goal in question exists in a clear and explicit manner somewhere. That is the case here: in the first example the goal appears frequently in Tim's consciousness, and in the second it exists similarly in the director's consciousness, and can also be seen in an e-mail message. To paraphrase Rubinstein, in these cases we can pinpoint an episode of having a goal in (someone's) consciousness.

3. A cat stopped eating when it was satisfied.
4. A thermostat keeps the temperature between 18 and 21 degrees

With these two cases it sounds reasonable to talk about goals: if we notice that certain activity stops every time a certain state is reached, it is natural to call that state a "goal". It is reasonable to say that the cat's goal was to satisfy hunger, and the goal of the thermostat's was to keep the temperature between 18 and 21°C. It is also possible to describe and pinpoint the mechanisms that give rise to the activity that appears as goal-orientated. The cat's consciousness presumably contains phenomenal states on the goal of its behaviour. However, in the fourth example, the goal does not exist anywhere, and one might claim that the talk about it is misleading—we should think that behaviour just *appears as goal-orientated*.

5.   Computers update their anti-virus programmes in order to avoid infections.
6.   Bees make honey in order to survive over winter.

Again, activities appear as goal-directed and the goal cannot be pinpointed from the organism/apparatus. Here, similar to the previous cases, there is also a *disposition to engage in certain activities* (cf. Rubinstein, 1997). In the fifth example, the apparent goal-directness (as-if intentionality) derives from the goal that once was in the programmer's consciousness. Behind the apparent goal-directness (as-if intentionality) in example six, there is the logic of evolution: if a behavioural disposition increases the fitness of a species, it becomes more prevalent. And bees survive because they make honey.

The questions to which Darwin's evolutionary theory was the answer can be seen as follows:

> In the nineteenth century biologists were exercised by the question of how matter could be organized into systems which subserved a goal, without citing explanation by final causes or calling on vital forces or divine purpose to explain the self-regulation of living systems. [Braddock, 2006, p. 402]

Evolutionary theory is able to tell us why certain traits of species have become common, and—as we noticed—the evolutionary viewpoint holds with behavioural dispositions, too. It has been found that men, regardless of culture, race, religion, or ethnicity, rate women with waist–hip ratio 0.7 (waist circumference being 70% of the hip circumference) as the most attractive. The (evolutionary) logic behind that is the following: women with such waist–hip ratio are most healthy and fertile, and thus they are also more likely give birth to offspring. Consequently, men attracted to women with 0.7 waist–hip ratio breed more effectively than other men. On this basis we can state that men's interest in those women possesses an (evolutionary) function of increasing the fitness of a species.

Thus, around the women with such a waist–hip ratio we see a lot of behaviour that appears goal-directed. Partly, that behaviour really is goal-directed: when trying to appeal to those women, men have certain goals in their consciousnesses. However, the *goal of increasing fitness* does not appear there. Actually, such a goal does not exist anywhere, because, strictly speaking, the process of evolution has no goals. Behaviour related to fitness possesses an evolutionary *function*, but it is merely apparently goal-directed.

Empirical research of unconscious goals and "the new unconscious"

Since the 1990s, cognitive unconscious has become more ecologically valid when metacognition, affect, and motivation have been taken under scrutiny. John Bargh's study from the year 1990 introduced the idea of non-conscious motives and goals. Bargh created a model that he calls the "auto-motive model of nonconscious goal pursuit". According to this, intentions and goals are represented in memory in the same way as stereotypes and schemas, and they may become activated non-consciously (see, for example, Chartrand & Bargh, 2002).

Social psychologists, having got stuck on these issues (Bargh among them), talk about "the new unconscious". In the Introduction to the book *The New Unconscious* (Hassin, Uleman, & Bargh, 2005), one of the editors (Uleman) tells us that the new unconscious is basically the "old" cognitive unconscious applied to the new topics.

Gordon Moskowitz, for example, has shown that a conscious ideal also affects unconscious processes. Behind Moskowitz, Gollwitzer, Wasel, and Schaal's (1999) study there is the empirical fact that stereotypic connections between stimuli speed up information processing: when the word "sensitive" (a stereotypical trait of women; in this kind of empirical setting such a stimulus is called the "target") is preceded 200 milliseconds earlier by a flash of a woman's picture (the "prime"), the word is read faster than if the picture were showing a man (so-called "automatic stereotype activation"). Moskowitz and his collaborators were able to show that this holds with "nonchronic egalitarians", but not with subjects having "chronic egalitarian goals". The crucial thing here is that the interval between the prime (the picture) and the target (the word) was so short that the subjects were not able to consciously process their ideals related to stereotyping—thus, the study indicates that an egalitarian attitude or goal may operate on the unconscious level, too.

Another study that may be called "classical" is that of Chartrand and Bargh (1996). In the first phase, subjects were asked to form a grammatically correct four-word sentence from five words presented in scrambled order (prime; so-called "the scrambled sentence test"). In the second phase, the participants read a series of sixteen behaviours (target). In the third phase, they were given a surprise free recall test. In the scrambled sentence test, half of the participants had words related to "impression formation goal" ("evaluate", "personality", "impression", "opinion"), and the other half words related to "memorization goal" ("remember", "memory", "retain", "absorb"). In turned out that those primed with an impression formation goal correctly recalled a greater number of behaviours.

The logic of the study depends on the empirical notion that "deep processing of information"—in this case "evaluating" matters and "creating impressions" on people—enhances memory performance. As a matter of fact, the study mirrors the classic study of Hamilton, Katz and Leirer (1980). They gave participants an explicit instruction to either form an impression, or to memorize the stories. Thus, when reading the stories, the participants had such a goals in their consciousness. Those encouraged to carry out deep processing ("form an impression") remembered the stories better. The logic behind Chartrand and Bargh's study is that through the scrambled sentence test the goals became activated non-consciously.

After the surprise free recall test, Chartrand and Bargh debriefed the participants. They state,

No participant showed any awareness or suspicion of a relation between the different tasks of the experiment or indicated that what he or she had done on one task might have affected how he or she had responded on another. In addition, no participant reported

having the intention either to memorize information or to form and
impression at any time during the experiment. [Chartrand & Bargh,
1996, p. 468]

Thus, the conclusion is that the goals became activated non-
consciously.

In order to legitimate the term "new", the researchers of the new
unconscious have to stress the differences between their approach
and the, say, "classic" view of the cognitive orientation. There are
grounds for such a distinction: ecological validity of the present-
day studies is better. However, we must ask if the new domain of
research is magnifying its significance when boldly talking about
non-conscious goals: we could easily explain the data without referring to goals at all; primes just make the participants adopt a certain
mode to process information (egalitarian or non-egalitarian, creating impressions, or memorizing).

The researchers of the new unconscious also make distinctions
in respect of psychoanalytic views. Uleman states that the "psychoanalytic unconscious" is ". . . widely acknowledged to be a failure
as a scientific theory because evidence of its major components
cannot be observed, measured precisely, or manipulated easily",
and that it "does not provide an influential framework for understanding unconscious processes in academic or scientific circles. . ."
(Uleman, 2005, p. 6).

Uleman describes the academic status of psychoanalytic views
correctly. Interestingly, he also states that, in the scope of the new
unconscious, "Goals, motives, and self-regulation are prominent,
without the conflict and drama of the psychoanalytic unconscious"
(ibid.). Uleman is right that in psychoanalytic parlance dramas are
projected into the unconscious. However, literally speaking, it is not
the unconscious that contains dramas, but life. If the researchers
took serial killers, for example, as the object of study, conflicts and
dramas would emerge at once. Here, the new unconscious carries
the inheritance of the old cognitive unconscious: the book *The New
Unconscious* does not treat more serious existential issues than that
of talking about the work problems in the party. Regardless of
whether the unconscious is taken to be "old" or "new", or "cognitive" or "psychoanalytic", dramas of human life should be placed
under scrutiny.

In a more profound study, the relation between the new unconscious and psychoanalytic views appears as rather complicated. John Kihlstrom, the inventor of the term "cognitive unconscious", states, ". . . the human mind is capable of maintaining unconscious vigilance over its own automatic processes. This suggests a volitional nature of the unconscious, an idea that to many may seem self-contradictory" (Glaser & Kihlstrom, 2005, p. 189). He also thinks that the unconscious is capable of holding "metacognitive processing goals", which it pursues "through self-monitoring". He draws the conclusion "This thesis . . . represents a departure from traditional conceptions of the unconscious as passive and reactive, suggesting an unconscious that is, paradoxically, 'aware'" (*ibid.*, p 190). This sounds like Freud modernizing his idea of censorship.

From the Freudian cornerstone to the Freudian phenomena

In Chapter Three, the Freudian view of the unconscious was studied in a profound manner, and especially its ontological presuppositions were scrutinized. It appeared that the Freudian view is confused, and that it contradicts that of present-day science in a foundational manner. In this chapter we have studied the influence of unconscious matters on different kinds of activities on a more general level. Surprisingly, present-day views of cognitive neuroscience appear to provide strong support for Freudian insights—psychoanalysts' clinical observations can be explained rather well by leaning on the research and models put forward in the domain of cognitive neuroscience.

When a negative attitude towards psychoanalysis joins together with a detailed study of psychoanalytic ideas and a biased selection of topics, we get a Freud-as-a-villain picture. Correspondingly, a positive attitude, scrutiny on a more general level, and a biased selection of topics lead one to the conclusion that Freud was a genius whose ideas have later turned out to be correct to an astonishing extent. These pictures are both distorted, since they emerge from, say, a "Freud-centred world-view"—Freud-bashing reflects such a view as well as his idealization.

If one aims to present a realistic picture, it is difficult to avoid being driven to endless Freud wars. Those wars are exciting, but (at least for me) it is more appealing to set aside the status of Freud's views and concentrate on what is the best way to study and conceptualize certain (Freudian) phenomena. The considerations made so far legitimate at least the following remarks on this.

First, neuroscientific models—treated above in terms of unconscious detections and unconscious neural algorithms (implicit knowledge)—shed light on the neural basis of matters such as transference, defences, and apparently goal-orientated behaviour in general. Instincts can also be treated in that frame. They are general behavioural dispositions that become realized in certain situations and environments. Detection of an object that may satisfy an instinct or desire is the meeting-point of an inner urge and an environment. Second, empirical research put forward in the scope of the study of the "new unconscious" indicates that rather complicated procedures may be generated outside the scope of consciousness. Third, the logic behind evolutionary biologists' talk about evolutionary functions of traits can be applied to the psychoanalytic idea of repressive functions of acts and ideas. (This matter is studied in detail in the Chapter Six.)

For a clinician, these matters do not necessarily possess factual relevance. Empirical research of psychology in general, and thus also the study put forward in the domain of the new unconscious, deals with more or less common characteristics of humans (nomothetic study). In contrast to that, psychoanalysts and psychoanalysis focus on individuals' personal life (idiographic study). Most statements of psychoanalysis will never be tested empirically, and statistical truths would not even be helpful for clinicians. This holds, of course, with all other clinical theories. The picture is wholly different when we approach the cognitive–neuroscience perspectives introduced above in terms of the scientific status of psychoanalysis.

Rubinstein (1997, pp. 43–66) has posited that theoretical terms of psychoanalysis are—or should be—*proto-neurophysiological*. By that he means that the psychoanalytic theory cannot be anchored to neurophysiological facts, but its terms should nevertheless be reasonable and possible from the perspective of neurosciences— when current views of neuroscience contradict psychoanalytic ideas, psychoanalytic models have to be amended. In this spirit we can say that psychoanalytic terms should also be *proto-empirical*— they should not contradict empirical study.

Scientific models always contain speculative aspects, and Edelman and Tononi (2000, p. 178), too, grant that their model concerning unconscious neural routines is near to "speculative neurology". We must endure speculative tones and study how Edelman's and others' models and empirical studies of the unconscious might help us to model psychoanalysts' clinical notions in terms of the two-sphere view.

Mathew H. Erdelyi (for example, 2006) has claimed that repressed ideas have always been previously conscious, and that Freud, too, thought that way. It is irrelevant to dispute Freud's actual view here, since adopting Erdelyi's view anyway has an important consequence—it simply solves the contradiction between psychoanalysis and other domains of study. That is, in the proto-neurophysiological and proto-empirical spirit, there are good reasons to presuppose that, for example, conscious efforts to control distressing aggressive and sexual ideas may become automatized. We learn to anticipate such topics unconsciously, since the human brain is able to detect which "stimuli"—words and tones of voice, for example—often precede distressing conscious states. Hearing a word related to a distressing topic might, for example, make us automatically—without conscious decision—turn the discussion to other topics.

Thus, clinical phenomena that psychoanalysts have been used to conceptualize through the expression "repressed desire" should be seen in terms of conscious goals that, for the first, have become automatized, and for the second, have been forgotten to have existed. The distinction between *non-conscious* goals and *repressed* ones can be made as follows: in the former case the episode(s) of having had the goal in consciousness can usually be remembered if necessary, but in the latter case there are specific (psychodynamic) reasons for not remembering it.

This chapter began with a short study on memory. It was stated that, with remembering, we deal with construction: memories are not stored as such in the brain. Instead, memory performances are based on several conscious and non-conscious processes. The above considerations on motives, goals, and desires lead us to the same conclusion: in the brain there are no goals or desires, and the ones appearing in the domain of consciousness have been constructed there.

On this basis we should approach the phenomenon of repression by thinking that when a certain desire does not exist in the scope of consciousness, although it should, certain constructive processes have been inhibited—a repressed content is not "hiding" in the unconscious, but a content has been prevented from becoming formed in the scope of consciousness. In the following chapter, repression and becoming conscious of the repressed is studied from that perspective.

CHAPTER FIVE

Repression and becoming conscious of the repressed reframed: the four-level model

I n psychoanalytic communities there are surely ideological reasons for tending towards the three-sphere view. There is also a practical reason: the cornerstone provides guidelines for psychoanalysts' work. The aim of psychoanalysis and psychodynamic therapies has been seen as making the repressed conscious— bringing repressed contents from the unconscious part of the mind into the scope of consciousness. If there is no mental unconscious, that rationale collapses.

Chapter Three pinpointed the problems of the three-sphere view: no one has ever said what those unconscious contents are actually like, and where and how they exist. In Chapter Four we examined the possibility that repressed memories and desires were stored by the brain. That line of thought was demonstrated to be a dead-end. The obvious logical conclusion is that when ideas are missing from consciousness, they are not "hiding" anywhere, but are prevented from being formed in the domain of consciousness.

According to my knowledge, no one has ever spelled out this "third way" in detail. This is related to a common failure to make the distinction between data (clinical observations; *explanadum*) on one hand, and the theories aiming at explain the data (*explanada*) on the other. It is rarely noted that the following three claims are *not* observations: (a) there are repressed ideas, (b) in the beginning of psychotherapy certain ideas are repressed, and (c) towards the end of psychotherapy a therapist can often notice that some repressed ideas have become conscious. Instead, they are *theory-laden descriptions* on the process of psychotherapy.

When studying the actual observations, it has to be noted that, a century after Freud's first writings, we are not restricted to *psychoanalytic* clinical data any more: currently, the field of psychotherapy consists of numerous branches. Present-day cognitive psychotherapy (or especially cognitive–constructive psychotherapy) is quite near to the psychodynamic model—therapy may even last for several years. Several branches of both psychodynamic and cognitive therapies have made the following two claims. First, patients possess distorted, biased, or unrealistic ideas on their life history, desires, and significant others. Patients' ideas are not unrealistic merely accidentally, but in a systematic manner. Second, during a successful therapy, some of the ideas change to more realistic or appropriate ones. In the scope of psychodynamic therapies, such a change is conceptualized in terms of repression, and cognitive therapists talk about distorted information processing strategies, for example.

The difference in conceptualization is due to the differences in background theories and therapeutic techniques. There is surely room for debate between cognitive and psychoanalytic views. Anyway, for current purposes, the crucial thing is the shared clinical notion concerning the change that takes place in the course of therapy: some of the patients' unrealistic ideas become replaced by more accurate ones. This is the phenomenon that Freud noticed at the end of the nineteenth century, and that should be approached in terms of current views of behavioural sciences. Let us stress that this phenomenon is on no account restricted to the clinical context of psychotherapy: in daily life we find repeatedly our own and others' predisposition to treat one's personal characteristics, desires, envies, and fears in a biased manner.

On the one hand there are clinical and daily observations on repression, and on the other hand there is the conventional psychoanalytic explanation of it, based on the problematic three-sphere view. There is the danger that the phenomenon of repression (and becoming conscious of the repressed) remains a prisoner of the three-sphere view and Freud wars. With Hannu Tiitinen (Talvitie & Tiitinen, 2006), I took hold of this danger and created a *the four-level model* of repression. It approaches repression in terms of the two-sphere view, and makes the "third way" explicit. It also provides theoretically sound foundations for the psychoanalysts' rationale of making the repressed conscious.

The four-level model

The starting point of the four-level model is the cognitivist idea that conscious states are always the *end-products of several neural and conscious processes*. Thus, the absence of an idea from consciousness means that some of those processes have not taken place, and when one possesses unrealistic ideas, those processes have occurred in a distorted manner. We claimed that those processes have to be studied in terms of four levels: (neural processes of) the brain, consciousness, self-consciousness, and narrative self-consciousness.

As mentioned, the four-level model emerges from the cognitive tradition, and it sounds rather familiar for one acquainted with the term *metacognition*, and fits well with Fred Dretske's (1995, pp. 39–63) view on introspection. Interestingly, when approaching the unconscious 100 years ago, Hugo Münsterberg (mentioned in the third chapter), had a basic orientation that comes quite near to the four level model (see Münsterberg, 1909, pp. 125–157). The model has predecessors also in the psychoanalytic tradition (for references, see Talvitie & Tiitinen, 2006, p. 171). Peter Fonagy and Mary Target have recently created an approach in which human development, psychopathology, and psychotherapeutic techniques are studied through the term *mentalization* (see Allen & Fonagy, 2006). The four-level model resonates strongly with the idea of mentalization—it can be seen as an elaboration and extension of Fonagy's and Target's view. Let us now turn to the levels of processing.

Level 1: Neurophysiological processes

In our brains there is massive neural activity at every moment. It makes no sense to think that some part of that activity is conscious and the rest remains unconscious. Instead, we should hold that neural activity *gives rise* to conscious states. Thus, when studying the processes that lead to a formation of a particular content of consciousness, neural processes lie at the bottom.

The previous chapter studied the competencies of the (unconscious) brain through the concepts of unconscious detection and neural algorithm. It is needless to broaden the landscape here—it is enough to state that, in terms of the four-level model, the unconscious is only the brain and its neural processes.

The Freudian view concerning consciousness and the unconscious can be said to be *digital*: ideas and mental states are either conscious or unconscious/repressed (the term preconscious does not change the picture very much). With the four-level model, we aimed at criticizing such a strict dichotomy in particular, suggesting that consciousness and the unconscious should be seen in an *analogical* manner: they are not alternatives, but form a continuum. We are not *either* conscious *or* not conscious on matters, but *less or more* conscious. This issue becomes evident along with the following considerations on consciousness, self-consciousness, and narrative self-consciousness.

Level 2: Consciousness

Conscious processing is linear, which means that there is just one process running at a time. In contrast to that, unconscious processes of the brain are parallel. Thus, from the economical and evolutionary perspectives, it is reasonable to process information unconsciously as much as possible. This leads us to ask why there is a need to process information consciously at all—what is the function of consciousness and conscious processing? Unconscious processing is rather mechanical, and novel problems cannot be solved in its scope. According to a prevalent view (see, for example, Baars, 1997), consciousness enables us to draw together information processed by the distinct modules of the brain. Consciousness is like a (global) workspace—as Baars states it—in the scope of which different kinds of sensory information is related to memories and one's knowledge.

Neural processes of the brain give rise to ideas, feelings, and associations. When studying the phenomenon of repression, it is, however, more revealing to state that the brain gives rise to a *stream of consciousness*. It makes a considerable difference whether an idea or feeling takes part in the stream for 200 milliseconds, or a minute, not to mention hours and days. So, when an idea or a feeling rapidly appears in the scope of consciousness, it is probably not remembered later. Thus, from the perspective of one's self-understanding, it makes no difference whether an idea has never appeared in consciousness, or if it appeared there for one fleeting moment. The mechanism that picks up particles from the stream of consciousness for closer examination is *attention*. Attention may also be directed to one's bodily reactions, and affairs taking place in the surrounding world.

According to the golden rule of psychoanalysis, the analysand should mention everything that comes to his or her mind. However, often many things come to mind, and the analysand has to choose which path to follow: even when the analysand is willing to report everything, he or she cannot. Feelings, mental images, and the specific meanings of things also often vanish rapidly from the consciousness. Thus, when the analysand is uneasy with a certain idea or feeling, attention rapidly turns away from that. Let me emphasize that I do not mean that the analysand *decides* to turn attention to other things. Instead, non-attending should be seen as a defence mechanism operating unconsciously. Let us call that *defensive (unconscious) non-attending*.

Level 3: Self-consciousness

Current mainstream views are more sensitive to different aspects of consciousness than the psychoanalytic conception—distinctions between varieties of conscious states are made through such terms as "minimal consciousness", "core consciousness", "self-consciousness", "conceptual self-consciousness", "reflective consciousness", "extended consciousness", "iterative meta-representational self-consciousness", "meta-self-awareness", and so on (see Morin, 2006). There are also the terms "phenomenal consciousness" and "access-consciousness" (Chalmers, 1996, pp. 25–31). The former term refers to the qualitative aspect of consciousness—our pains and pleasures—whereas the latter deals with the fact that when we are in one conscious state, we might or might not be aware of other states.

The meaning and significance of matters emerge only when distinct memories and facts are accessible at one and the same time. For example, as such it is not news that one's female friend is drinking only mineral water in the restaurant. However, if the fact of how a mother's use of alcohol may affect the foetus is accessible for the friend, who has ordered a beer, ordering mineral water takes on a new significance.

Restriction of access to consciousness is an everyday phenomenon. When concentrating on writing, for example, bodily signs of hunger are not necessarily accessible for one, and when trying to score a goal in a football game, one might not notice a painful wound in a leg. As we see, many competencies are based on restricting access to consciousness—it is a presupposition for so-called "flow experiences".

In the domain of psychiatry and psychoanalysis, restriction of access between conscious states is called dissociation. It is possible that, in some cases, the phenomenon of repression is actually dissociation: what appears as repressed in one situation—for example, that of psychoanalytic hour—may be conscious in the other. Actually, empirical research strongly supports the idea that repression is, in this way, context-dependent (Rofé, 2008).

There is also the distinction between consciousness and self-consciousness. A fish is conscious of another fish swimming in front of it, and an infant is conscious of the light being switched off. Fish and infants possess conscious states, but they are not self-conscious beings: they do not possess ideas on their personal characteristics (sex, age, unique life history, idiosyncratic ways of reacting to stimuli, etc.), do not know what their current feelings are compared to those they had yesterday, and they do not understand that their life is finite.

For the most part, defences should be seen as restricting access between conscious states, memories, and feelings, and thus operating on the level of self-consciousness. When hearing tragic news, we sometimes react extremely inappropriately, such as by staying calm, or even laughing hysterically. In such a case we know the facts: my spouse is dead; I will never talk with her any more; all our plans for the future will never be realized, and so on. Inappropriate reaction means that one has not been able to comprehend the personal (or emotional) significance of the facts. More theoretically, we might say that the facts have not been integrated to one's narrative self.

People behaving impulsively in a violent manner often say that something "just clicked in my head": they cannot identify the relation between the violent outburst and the matters that preceded it. However, one would not have acted violently if those matters had not possessed an insulting meaning. Thus, the person has consciously detected the insulting matter. When the person cannot name the insult afterwards, it is because access to the conscious state preceding the violent act is restricted. When a person sincerely claims that there was just "a click in the head", it means that he or she did not, and do not, attend to the ideas and feelings that preceded the outburst—there is defensive non-attending at work. Dissociation and non-attending are also of help in not facing the implication of the outburst: "I'm a person that cannot tolerate certain insulting things".

The above considerations on self-consciousness and the access aspect of conscious states make it clear that conscious states do not just pop up—they develop along with neural and conscious processes. There are ideas and conscious states that are less and more sophisticated, and complex states/ideas emerge when more primitive ones are combined in the scope of the workspace of consciousness. When one does not attend to his or her feelings and bodily reactions, and does not study the logic of associations (stream of consciousness), certain sophisticated ideas/states do not become formed in the scope of consciousness. The above example on violent outbursts illustrates that, but let us take one more example.

I feel envious towards Alan because his handicap in golf is eight. That sophisticated state presupposes at least three more primitive states/ideas. First, my desire to be a good golfer, which means achieving a low handicap. Second, the notion that Alan is a good golfer. And third, a comparing notion, accompanied by a certain feeling that Alan has or is something that I do not/am not.

A psychoanalyst may consider that the above examples of golf and the mental life of fish are rather superficial, and that psychoanalysts study deeper layers of the mind. Throughout this book I have deliberately used simple examples, so that the reader does not need to accept psychoanalytic doctrines in order to follow the logic of the text. Focusing on the Oedipus complex, for example, would not change the picture, however. In terms of the four-level model, the story about repressed oedipal wishes would go as described below.

One has fleeting sexual and aggressive feelings towards parents, but they break away from consciousness without closer examination—the person in question does not attend to them, and thus they are not accessible (remembered) for him or her later. There are also fantasies (fears) on how the parent of the same sex might suffer an accident, for example. According to the golden rule of psychoanalysis, the analyst should mention everything that comes to his or her mind. This means that attention becomes directed also to those sexual and aggressive feelings. The analyst or the analysand him/herself may draw together those feelings, the fantasies, and a certain oedipal logic of association by claiming that one has (had) repressed oedipal ideas. Thus, oedipal interpretation should be seen as a construction on several matters having taken place in psychoanalysis.

Level 4: Narrative self-consciousness

When language(s) developed some tens of thousands of years ago, it triggered a considerable change in human nature. It enabled us to code and store information, and transfer it to another. Language also gave rise to abstract thinking, and we became able to create fictive worlds. With the help of language it was possible to apprehend oneself and others in new ways—as beings possessing certain mental characteristics and unique personal history. If we studied repression without paying special attention to language, we would approach the phenomenon as it may have appeared in *homo erectus*. It is important to remind oneself that language is also the domain in which psychoanalytic psychotherapy (mostly) takes place.

Let us note two things here. First, in this chapter the focus has shifted from the brain towards meanings. Focusing on meanings, symbols, language, and narration also means a shift from the scope of neuroscience and natural science towards the domain of humanities (or hermeneutics). Second, the above considerations on self-consciousness were, in a certain sense, misleading. Strictly speaking, examples of ordering mineral water, Alan's golfing handicap, and so on do not fall in the scope of pure, non-verbal self-consciousness, since they presuppose language and abstractions.

Narrative psychoanalysis (see, for example, Schafer, 1992) has focused on the role of language and narration in psychoanalytic practice and theorizing. It is founded on the works of three respected philosophers: Paul Ricoeur's (1970) book, *Freud and Philosophy: An Essay on Interpretation*, Jürgen Habermas's chapter, "The scientistic self-misunderstanding of metapsychology", in *Knowledge and Human Interests* (1968, pp. 246–273), and Ludwig Wittgenstein's remarks on psychoanalysis (see Bouveresse, 1991). The following considerations on language are based on those works, and affected by Georg Henrik von Wright's ideas as presented in the book *In the Shadow of Descartes: Essays in the Philosophy of Mind* (von Wright, 1998).

Brain imaging methods have recently developed greatly, and we are constantly told news that neuroscientists have found neural correlates for a certain psychic illness or a personal trait. Conscious states and verbal expression surely have their counterparts in the brain, too. Consciousness and language cannot, however, be *reduced* to neurophysiological matters—they cannot be seen as just epiphenomena, side-effects of the brain, but rather as mental tools that make a radical difference to the human essence.

The previous chapter referred to Michael Spivey stating that we are bad at describing our mental states verbally: one "hate" word refers to a number of different phenomenal and neural states. The notion that verbal expressions of mental matters are always culture-dependent takes us still further from the world of natural science.

As Habermas and, especially, Wittgenstein stress, each language community has its own vocabulary for mental matters, and we have all been socialized to adopt the folk psychology of the surrounding culture. When studying language as a social phenomenon, we find that its function is less to represent the state of things objectively, and more to make things happen in the social world. Consequently, our verbal expressions of our mental states are not true or false at first hand. Instead, they are more or less realistic or appropriate given the data, and the conventions prevailing in one's language community. We cannot deny that sentences and stories describe the world around and inside us. However, language is far from a neutral or objective way to make pictures of the world.

All in all, a rather confusing picture of language emerges: (1) verbal expressions possess neural correlates but—at least in the present context—neuroscientific studies do not shed light on the meanings and use of language; (2) it is possible to describe mental states verbally, but those descriptions are rather inexact; (3) language is a cultural phenomenon, and cultural conventions provide the frames, and also set the limits, in which we talk about our phenomenal reality.

Words and sentences form webs of meanings—each word has several meanings, and a sentence or a story may be interpreted in a variety of ways—and language enables us to build an abstract model of the world in our minds. It seems that we should approach language as a domain of its own—one which, however, has intimate connections to neurophysiological, phenomenal, and cultural matters.

The above viewpoints carry two implications, both extremely significant for our topic. First, the idea that we possess an inner (neural and/or phenomenal) reality that just becomes expressed through words and sentences is fundamentally flawed.

Second, psychoanalytic clinical data is not about consciousness of contents. The three-sphere view of psychoanalysis has caused us to think that ideas might be either conscious or unconscious (repressed), and that psychoanalysts are in a position to make observations on that. Strictly speaking, this is not the case. We can know only our *own* conscious states, and thus psychoanalysts have knowledge of their analysands' contents of consciousness only as far as the analysands report them. From the epistemological point of view, we must note that a psychoanalyst cannot know that a certain idea is missing from the analysand's consciousness—he or she knows only that an idea is missing from the analysand's *narration*.

These viewpoints lead us to the following conclusion: repression, as it appears in the clinical context, should be seen as a phenomenon that takes place in the scope of narration, and refers to one's narrative self-consciousness.

When introducing the term "self", there is the danger of falling into deep philosophical considerations: does such a "thing" as a self exist, and if it does, what actually is it; do animals and computers have a self, and so on. The psychoanalytic three-sphere view contains confusing ontological presuppositions, and it would be a mistake to just replace them with another set of confusing presuppositions. Daniel Dennett (1989; Dennett & Humphrey, 1989) treats narrative self as a phenomenon that becomes created through language. Narrative self is a picture that is painted when "one tells stories about him or herself". More technically, it can be determined as the whole of the ideas about oneself that one has verbalized, silently or aloud, and that one currently is able to retrieve from memory.

We can explicitly state that "I am humble", for example, but most of our statements and stories we tell just *imply* something about ourselves. When one talks about Mahatma Gandhi, Unicef, Rocky movies, or full-contact karate in a respectful or enthusiastic manner, he or she tells us something about him or herself. If talking enthusiastically about all of them, there seems to be a contradiction in the air. A person who likes golf, Karlheinz Stockhausen's compositions, and Fyodor Dostoyevsky's novels is surely quite different from another who appreciates ice hockey, Dire Straits, and Raymond Chandler. Similarly, the things we desire and fear always imply something about us as persons—we do not just happen to work hard for career development, an admired title, or a lower handicap in golf. Such an interdependence of the meanings (of ideas) is called *mental* or *semantic holism*. When we see the narrative self this way, philosophical problems are avoided: it is not supposed to be an entity located in our minds, but a theoretical concept that refers to a portrait that each of us draws by talking.

The scientific community has had mixed reactions towards Freudian notions on repression and the unconscious, partly due to the Freudian presuppositions behind those concepts. However, there is a consensus that humans have tendencies to see (and narrate) themselves in one way, and resistance to that in certain other ways. This can be restated by saying that our cognitions and narratives on ourselves are often biased. In the domain of social psychology, Hazel Markus laid the ground for the study of self, self-image, and self-schema, and, during the past decade, cognitive neuroscience has shown growing interest in the topic of self (see Gallagher & Shear, 1999; Tesser, Stapel, & Wood, 2002). Neuroscientists are currently able to tell, for example, which areas of the brain are associated with self-related cognition (Gusnard, 2005).

Dennett (1991, p. 418) holds that the self has to be controlled, protected, and defined, and this occurs through telling stories of what one is like. According to him, the boundaries of our selves also change: "sometimes we enlarge our boundaries; at other times, in response to perceived challenges real or imaginary, we let our boundaries shrink" (*ibid.*, p. 417). Dennett's idea sounds quite familiar here. It can be put in a psychoanalytic way by stating that we have an ideal self or self-image that might become threatened, and a threat gives rise to resistance and activates defences.

The four-level model in practice

At the beginning of this chapter I emphasized that we must be careful about what is data/observations and what is theory, i.e., an effort to explain the former. The clinical data around repression is that certain ideas or topics are systemically missing from the narration: the analysand does not mention certain ideas, topics, desires, feelings, and fears, that he or she presumably possesses. According to the Freudian idea, those matters exist in the (mental or neural) unconscious, and verbalization of an idea indicates that it has become conscious. The four-level model paints a different picture, and enables us to treat the Freudian phenomena (observations) in terms of present-day views of different branches of study and the two-sphere view.

As we have seen, the contents of consciousness should be regarded as emerging along with several neural and mental processes: (1) neural processes of the brain; (2) conscious processes; (3) processes on the level of (non-verbal) self-consciousness; and (4) narrative self-consciousness, i.e., inner speech and audible verbalizations, that do the same as (3) but in a more sophisticated manner. Consequently, an absence of content is due to the missing of processes on one or several of those levels. According to this logic, repression appears so that missing ideas are prevented from being formed. Behind an absence of ideas (from consciousness and/or narration), repression, and defence mechanisms there are the three cornerstones of the four-level model: unconscious detections, unconscious neural algorithms, and selective non-attending.

Verbalized contents of consciousness should be seen as *constructions*. When using that term I am not trying to say that verbalizations of mental states were *just* constructions. When someone is going to give a talk in an auditorium, and his hands tremble and distressing memories of past public appearances flood into his mind, it is extremely plausible, realistic, and accurate to claim that he is nervous and afraid of failure. However, it is also possible to deny that. In that case, the fear of failure does not lie in the unconscious. Instead, one either does not attend to the trembling of hands and associations to past failures (i.e., one is not self-conscious of them), or denies the fact that in one's linguistic community such phenomenal and behavioural matters are held to refer to the fear of failure.

Let us consider an analysand who habitually misses, or is late for, the analytic hours preceding the analyst's vacation. The analysand thinks that this reflects no more than a series of unfortunate events: there were unexpected traffic jams, for example. The analyst, however, cannot think that way. Instead, he holds that the analysand is repressing something: perhaps the situation contains the unconscious meaning that the analyst is rejecting the analysand. Or maybe the pre-vacation situation activates certain childhood memories: for the analysand, the analyst's one-sided notification about the vacation reflects a sadistic and controlling tendency, which characterized her father. Thus, the analyst thinks that behind the missing of pre-vacation sessions there is repressed rage.

The sentence "the analysand has missed pre-vacation sessions because of repressed rage" does not express a neural or mental fact: we cannot pinpoint from the brain or (unconscious) mind an entity (of rage) that has made the analysand miss sessions. On the other hand, it is not credible to state (in the linguistic community that both the analyst and the analysand belong to) that missing several pre-vacation sessions during the past three years is just chance. According to the commonsense psychology of the linguistic community, behind the missing of sessions there has to be a conscious or unconscious intention, desire, fear, or aim. The point is that, in a similar way to the impulsive and violent person defensively non-attending to certain matters, the analysand refuses to study missing sessions, say, realistically. If someone else had missed sessions in that way, the analysand would say right away that change does not explain the matter.

Thus, from this perspective, repression appears as selective and biased processing of phenomenal and behavioural data. Refusing to study matters realistically, and leaning on unbelievable explanations ("click in the head", "traffic jams . . ."), should be seen as efforts to guard the narrative self: the matters behind violence and the missing of sessions are such that they would violate it.

In psychoanalysis and psychoanalytic therapy, the aim is to make the repressed conscious. In terms of the four-level view, that means that it supports the processes that would lead to the emergence of the missing contents of narrative self-consciousness. Thus, the process of psychotherapy simulates, or mirrors, the process of the making of a verbalized conscious state. Consequently, therapists' functions and activities can also be expressed in terms of the four-level view as described below.

The level of the brain and neural processes has only minor importance in psychotherapy: a therapist does not try to change the brain in order to allow access to the missing contents, but the brain is encouraged to change through talking. However, in certain cases, it is recommended that drugs should be combined with psychotherapy. In terms of the four-level view, this is to be conceptualized so that a neurophysiological intervention makes a depressive patient's brain produce a more lively stream of consciousness.

Both psychoanalytic and cognitive practitioners hold that the core issue in therapy is to focus on patients' states of consciousness and bodily feelings. Therapists present interpretations, but before the time is right for these, data—a patient's feelings, memories, associations, and so on—have to be collected. Patients produce that data, but therapists also have a role to play through questions and suggestions: "How do you feel now/about that", for example. When asking such a question, a therapist acts as, say, an external mechanism of attention. He or she does something that the patient's own mechanism of attention has left undone: directs sight to conscious states and bodily reactions in order to draw them into the scope (or workspace) of self-consciousness. (To be exact, we should talk about *narrative* self-consciousness, since attending occurs through a verbal request.)

When a therapist says "This reminds me of . . .", or "Perhaps this has something to do with the dream you told me last time", his or her function is similar to the general function of (self-)consciousness: to bring together ideas and experiences that appear as distinct, yet are not.

Narrative self-consciousness is self-evidently at the core of psychotherapy, the "talking-cure": psychotherapists in general promote *verbalizing* matters. Feelings are named; ideas, desires, fears, and fantasies are given a linguistic form; tendencies and behavioural dispositions are constructed; a more nuanced narration on one's life-history is created. All this means that, in the course of psychotherapy, a patient's narrative self-consciousness becomes enriched: a patient later remembers (at least part of) the notions he or she has formed in a session.

Articulating matters that way leads, paradoxically, to more nuanced internal conflicts and contradictions: the violent person faces the insulting matters, and that challenges his or her belief of being a strong and peace-loving person; the analysand missing pre-vacation sessions feels the rage towards sadistic and controlling people. There is also good news. When psychic troubles become mechanically triggered through unconscious detections, unconscious neural algorithms, and defensively non-attended conscious states, they cannot be "handled". In contrast to that, when the troubles—in psychoanalytic parlance they are called "intrapsychic conflicts"—can be made to appear in the form of insulting and contradictory ideas, it is possible to learn to manage them, and sometimes even to solve them.

In the scope of psychoanalysis, enriching the narrative self-consciousness is expressed by claiming that unconscious desires, meanings, and so on are made conscious. According to the logic of the four-level model, we should think first that neural matters (unconscious detections and neural loops) lacking meanings are "mentalized" and become expressed in the scope of linguistic system, and second, non-attended mental matters possessing just primitive meanings become "full members" of the linguistic system.

The above considerations lack one extremely crucial issue: how does the brain "know" which ideas and feelings should be (defensively) non-attended and left non-verbalized? Considering the principles of the four-level model, the answer is obvious. We are able to unconsciously detect and recognize the dangerousness of matters, too. When we have experienced a traumatic situation, we are later able to unconsciously detect stimuli that are related to that situation, and the detection triggers (the unconscious neural algorithms of) defences.

Repression cannot, however, always be connected to traumatic events. It is often directed to a meaning that a certain act or perception does or does not contain—"Did you ask who I'm going to meet this evening because you are jealous?", for example. We may repress the meaning of a certain act or association implying that we are envious, sexually aroused, angry, or jealous, because that challenges our ego-ideal or narrative self. Thus, how do we know beforehand, and without conscious thinking, that attending to a meaning of a certain act and interrelating certain ideas would lead to a construction that challenges the narrative self?

In order to answer that question, let us note, first, that many of our competencies presume this kind of non-conscious knowledge: when riding a bicycle we know that certain movements would lead to our falling off, for example.

Second, when disputing familiar political, scientific, ethical, and practical issues, we are often able to present our counter-arguments immediately after (or even before) having heard the other person's statement. We understand the meaning of the statement and its relation to our own view immediately. Psychological issues concerning violence, being late, having desires and fears, being envious and jealous, and so on are extremely common to all of us: we have heard discussions on them since we learnt to understand speech, we have thought about them for thousands of hours, and we have read novels and seen films that treat such psychological topics. Thus, when a psychotherapist ask "How do you feel about that", or presents an interpretation, we know immediately the thematic landscape towards which the psychotherapist's comment is moving the discussion. If the landscape appears as threatening, unconscious defences might be triggered, or more or less conscious avoidance may take place.

When aiming at explaining matters around repression, perhaps we are liable to put too much weight on unconscious factors. I would ask the reader to consider a currently conscious matter that was previously repressed. What did you think at the moments of defensively avoiding the repressed idea? When repression has yielded in the course of psychotherapy, people often say, "Actually,

I have, in a certain way, always known those things". When we refuse to face our jealousy, for example, we often have a feeling rather difficult to describe—we deny an idea, but at the same time we somehow know that there is at least some truth in it, but we are very reluctant to study it more closely. This kind of notion shows that, in many cases, repression should be located between self-consciousness and narrative self-consciousness.

The mystery of the unconscious reconsidered

A cognitively-orientated reader does not long for further arguments in favour of the two-sphere view and the four-level model, and probably there are psychoanalytic folk that will not become convinced of *any* arguments that challenge the Freudian corner-stone. At the risk of boring all imaginable readers, I will study one possible counter-argument against the approach that I have sketched so far. The counter-argument concerns, say, the "spirit" of the four-level model.

In the scope of cognitive neuroscience, the unconscious is, non-dramatically, just the brain and its unconscious detections and neural algorithms, but psychoanalysts talk about the mysteries of the unconscious. Even the unconscious itself is often called a mystery, and psychoanalysts' work is thus held to occur on the edge of knowing and not-knowing. Analysands and analysts are both astonished at how the former's life history, early object-relations, and psychic troubles appear in a symbolic and metaphorical form in the analytic setting. Slips, dreams, and associations also seem to contain a logic that is somehow connected to the analysand's problems. Both participants find themselves thinking of unusual matters, and having strong and weird feelings towards each other. All in all, there are lots of phenomena that seem to possess a meaning, but that are not planned by either of the participants.

In the course of psychotherapy, some of these oddities can be made sense of, and some remain mysteries. These "psychoanalytic" experiences are so suggestive that analysts lean on the mystifying three-sphere view, although the logic behind it is confusing. Confusing theory somehow matches with confusing psychoanalytic experiences.

A psychoanalytically orientated reader may hold that the traditional psychoanalytic thinking describes our "inner reality" and "dynamics of the mind" more accurately or "deeply" than the two-sphere view and the four-level model. On this basis, he or she may claim that the four-level model, apart from sounding mechanical and technical, also does not reflect the vividness of clinical reality and our inner life.

The four-level view is aimed at providing an alternative for psychoanalytic models in particular, and weak spots of the latter are not arguments in favour of the four-level view. The four-level model has to stand on its own feet, and thus the (supposed) criticism concerning its lack of vividness (or a certain kind of ecological validity) has to be taken seriously—in addition to missing and emerging conscious states, the four-level view should be able to capture those "mysterious" phenomena, too.

There is a temptation to try to breathe some life into the four-level model, which originates in such a cool topic as artificial intelligence, very far from human passions. It is, however, more appropriate to take the opposite perspective and focus on the (supposed) vividness of psychoanalytic theorizing: in so far as psychoanalytic thinking is vivid, is it also true?

Behind the Freudian vividness there are some tricks, or, more generally speaking, a (Platonian) strategy of anthropomorphizing neural structures ("inner agents") and, say, "conscious-o-morphizing" unconscious processes. Suggestive talk about agencies such as ego, id, superego, and censorship easily leads the reader to forget that it refers to just neural structures and functions of the brain. When approaching the question "How does the unconscious mind 'know' which contents can be allowed to enter consciousness, and which should be repressed?", psychoanalysts tend to refer to Freud's views concerning censorship. However, that idea sounds bad: censorship appears as an agency capable of human-like thinking, and such an implication contains the so-called homunculus fallacy. Thus, the idea of censorship should be replaced by the model that shows how a system consisting of several sub-systems detects dangerousness of ideas, and triggers defence mechanisms. Such an approach does not sound vivid any more—there is a mechanical, cognitive-science clunk to it. The Hellenic way of talking about our behavioural dispositions—i.e., using the myths of Ancient Greece as examples—can also be seen as a rhetoric trick.

With this kind of narrative strategy, Freud makes the unconscious appear as vivid. If a cognitive neuroscience-inspired model like that of the four-level view sounds too cool for clinical purposes, it might be the case that actually it just lacks the Freudian rhetoric make-up.

* * *

In the first four chapters, we encircled the ontological issue of whether the unconscious should be held to be mental or just neural. In Chapter Four we also pondered whether the unconscious might contain entities such as memories, desires, goals (of behaviour), motives, wishes, intentions (or intentionality in general), and fears. With the ontological issue, I was led to a straightforward conclusion: the unconscious is plainly neural, and, strictly speaking, does not contain any of the entities listed above.

In this chapter, the focus turned from entities and contents to processes. I have suggested that, for the first, through unconscious detections and neural loops our acts and conscious states become affected by matters of which we are not conscious. For the second, the mechanism of defensive non-attending restricts the impact of perceptions, ideas, and feelings to our acts and narrative self-consciousness.

In this chapter a "linguistic turn" also took place. I argued that the Freudian cornerstone should be seen as an effort to comprise the issue that we always conceptualize and narrate our acts, desires, and fears, personal characteristics, phenomenal reality, and personal life history in a more or less distorted manner. Repression is less about keeping something completely outside consciousness, and more about restricting the impact of some phenomenal matters to our narrative self-consciousness.

The final chapter might be seen as an extension of that linguistic turn. In it, I study different kinds of discourses, perspectives, explanatory strategies, or "stances", through which it is possible to approach human behaviour and phenomenal reality. The core question is how a psychotherapist's thinking and talking is related to neuroscience, commonsense psychology, and scientific psychology. The perspective of this chapter makes—one more time—the Freudian cornerstone appear in a new light.

CHAPTER SIX

Psychotherapy, neuroscience, and the levels of explanation

Oxford Moral Sciences Club assembled on 25 October 1946, and during the gathering the only meeting of two giants of science took place. The encounter of those famous critics of psychoanalysis ended in a baleful atmosphere: Ludwig Wittgenstein, the chairman, threatened Sir Karl Popper, the lecturer, with a red-hot poker.

Wittgenstein, Popper, and Freud were all Vienna-born Jews. They are also closely connected to positivism: although Wittgenstein never participated in the meetings of the Vienna Circle, under the aegis of which positivism emerged, his early masterpiece *Tractatus Logico-Philosophicus* (Wittgenstein, 1922) was one of the core texts of it; Popper was a critic of positivism, who was never party to those meetings; together with Ernst Mach, Albert Einstein, and many others, Freud signed the call for the foundation of a "Society for Positivist Philosophy" in 1912, that was published also in *Zentralblatt für Psychoanalyse* (Vol. 3, 1912–1913, p. 56) (Fulgencio, 2005).

At the time of the meeting, Wittgenstein had already abandoned the ideas of the *Tractatus*. He had ended up thinking that philosophical problems are just puzzles that could be solved through a kind of philosophical therapy, comparable to psychoanalytic technique. Popper was prepared to challenge Wittgenstein's view—he argued that there are real philosophical problems, not just "puzzles". According to Popper, Wittgenstein challenged him to give an example of a moral rule, and at the same time handled a poker in a threatening manner. Popper's clever example was "not to threaten visiting lecturers with pokers". Furious, Wittgenstein reacted by throwing the poker down and storming out of the room, banging the door behind him.

According to the other participants of the meeting, things did not go exactly that way (see Edmonds & Eidinow, 2001). Anyway, the "Wittgenstein's poker" story illustrates that the critics of psychoanalysis do not form a monolith—psychoanalysis may be both attacked and advocated from several perspectives. Through the story we can also set the previous chapters in a context, and create a new one for this chapter.

In the preceding chapters, my perspective has mainly been empirical, "Popperian", in a general sense: I have critically studied the evidence and arguments in favour of the three-sphere view, and approached the mental unconscious in terms of ontology. It has become evident that no method of study has revealed the existence of the unconscious. Popper claimed that the core problem with psychoanalysis is that its presuppositions cannot be *falsified*. Thus, in the Popperian spirit, we might add that neither have psychoanalysts stated through which kind of experiment the three-sphere view might become falsified.

Late work by Wittgenstein focused on language and so-called language games. By talking about puzzles, Wittgenstein meant that philosophical problems arise from the misuse of language, and thus they could be cleared up by focusing on the correct use of concepts. His criticism towards psychoanalysis is not especially aggressive, and he considers psychoanalysis and the third-sphere concepts as ways of seeing and speaking (see Bouveresse, 1991). In the current chapter, the unconscious is examined from the perspective that is not Wittgensteinian, but its tone is nevertheless clearly more Wittgensteinian than Popperian—below the emphasis will be more practical than in the preceding chapters.

A psychotherapist's position: balancing existential and scientific challenges

One aspect of humans' existential challenge is to try to track down one's deepest aims, desires, and fears, and possess a relatively realistic idea of one's personal characteristics. Closely related to that challenge, we have problems that can be called existential troubles, psychic defects, and psychiatric disorders. It is extremely important to be able to deal with them both on the individual and institutional (public health, psychotherapy institutes) level. The existential challenge and those troubles are at the core of psychoanalysis as well as other psychotherapies—there are attempts to make theories on both psychic well-being and defects, and on this basis create psychotherapeutic "techniques" in order to help people to overcome their troubles.

It is reasonable to take a scientific stance towards these extremely personal matters: empirical study, scientific argumentation, and critique of fellow researchers enables us to create better theories and techniques. Evidently, it is highly desirable that psychotherapy should be based on scientific research and models

Psychotherapy contains also a practical and subjective (or private) side that is far from the scientists' laboratories. One might paraphrase Marx by stating that the aim of psychotherapy is not merely to explain our behaviour and experiences, but to change them. It is more than questionable that the best way to help oneself and others to deal with troubles is to adopt the most fashionable ideas of the philosophy of mind and neurosciences. When it comes to the former, a psychotherapist advocating eliminative materialism should perhaps be seen as repressing his or her own feelings, and thus unable to take seriously patients' despair and suffering. Concerning the latter, we might state that psychotherapy is intimate interaction between two persons, and neurophysiological education cannot posses a major role in it—knowledge of the neural correlates of one's troubles is rarely of help. The praxis of psychotherapy is bound to the concepts of commonsense psychology or "folk psychology" (of the surrounding culture), through which the therapist and the patient are used to express their feelings and ideas.

All in all, psychotherapists' work takes place on the edge: on the one hand each patient is different, possessing unique problems in his or her life, and thus a therapists cannot depend on manuals and studies that identify what kind of matters lie behind those troubles statistically. Moreover, a therapist's own personal characteristics possess a key role in therapy. On the other hand, therapists are supposed to base their interventions on scientific theories, and therapists themselves also long for firm foundations for their work.

In the previous chapters we have concentrated on the scientific problems around the unconscious. In practice, however, the concept is not especially problematic. In therapy and otherwise we occasionally facilitate insights such as "All my life I have tried to follow the advice and norms set by my parents without realizing that"; "The death of my sister cast a shadow over my childhood as well as my later life"; "Both my concentration on work and the problems with alcohol have actually been efforts to escape marital difficulties"; "I'm very competitive in most areas of life, and this originates in the relations with my father and brother"; "I have criticized Bob a lot, but as a matter of fact I have just been very envious of him". In such cases one has become conscious of something that was previously not conscious. In terms of (post-Freudian) commonsense psychology, it is entirely plausible to talk about repressed or unconscious fears, aims, and intentions.

In the preceding chapters I have criticized psychoanalysis for leaning on this kind of thinking, and created an alternative for psychoanalytic conceptualization. Paradoxically, for the most part it would be entirely absurd to talk about the "cornerstones" of that alternative (unconscious detections, unconscious neural loops, and defensive non-attending) in psychotherapy. It is not even evident that a psychotherapist should silently conceptualize therapeutic affairs using those terms—a psychotherapist is paid neither for true explanations nor scientifically correct use of terminology, but for promoting the well-being of his or her patients. A therapist's vocabulary and background theories are determined by practical considerations—the aims of psychotherapy.

A rather confusing picture emerges: the previous chapters indicate that the three-sphere view is simply erroneous, and that seems to imply that a psychoanalyst should not even think in terms of the psychoanalytic third-sphere concepts. However, the other options are far from tempting. On one hand, the concepts of commonsense psychology—in which a psychotherapist is bound in discussions with the patients—are surely no more scientific. On the other hand, the "scientific" terminology of neurosciences and philosophy of mind is mainly useless in the praxis of psychotherapy. From the scientific standpoint, it is intolerable that the relation between psychotherapists' thinking and scientific theories is coincidental. Thus, how to approach the practice of psychotherapy scientifically?

Below I aim to resolve this confusion. At first I will study the relations between commonsense psychology, the clinical vocabulary of psychotherapists, and that of neuroscience. Then I will take a look at the different kinds or levels of explanation.

Psychology, neuroscience, and the interface problem

Commonsense, or folk psychology has evolved in everyday interactions between people, and it is, similar to folk-physics, unscientific throughout. We have grown up thinking in terms of it—or one might say that commonsense psychology has bred us to think about psychological and social issues—and it is difficult to see what could be wrong with it. However, commonsense psychology is fragmentary and does not take a stand on certain core issues of academic psychology—for example, that concerning how knowledge is represented by the mind/brain. It presupposes that our desires and knowledge are like "sentences in the head" (propositional attitudes; "X believes/desires/fears A") but, as we have seen, actually we deal with distributed neural networks and population codes (for a rather theoretical view of the problems of commonsense psychology, see Dennett 1987, pp. 43–68).

When one—say, a Martian unfamiliar with the traffic issues on earth—asks "why did Tom brake very quickly after having seen something moving beside the road", the commonsense psychology explanation would go as follows: "Tom thought that the moving object might be a deer, for example, running towards the road. He knows that crashes with big animals are very dangerous, and in order to avoid a possible crash he braked".

Tom certainly knew that crashes are dangerous, but drivers in general do not think about such things all the time. Many reactions have become automatic: when a sign of danger is detected, automatic neural algorithms become triggered without conscious processing. Thus, when braking, Tom did not think what the object might be, what the crash with a big animal would mean, and how the crash could be avoided. We cannot escape the conclusion that as far as commonsense psychology is hold to tell what happens in one's mind/brain in a certain moment, it is simply erroneous.

We cannot, however, deny the fact that the above commonsense explanation is useful—it presents the *reason*, the *logic*, or the *function* of Tom's act. Thus, commonsense psychology is not "designed" to tell true stories on the *causes* of acts or what happens in one's mind/brain at a certain moment, but to *make sense* of behaviour. Let us also note that its predictive power is enormous: based on commonsense psychology we can quite often tell how a person will behave in a certain situation today, next week, or next year.

From the psychoanalytic perspective, commonsense psychology is untrustworthy due to its defensiveness: we often lack insight to our minds, and repress our factual desires. Folk-wisdom also contains weird ideas about child-breeding and appropriate "cures" for depression, among other things.

In most cases, scientific explanations cannot compete with the predictive power of commonsense psychology, and researchers concentrate on finding *why* such a non-scientific affair is so successful (see, for example, Gordon 1986; Horgan & Woodward, 1985). As mentioned, commonsense psychology is usually assumed to be able to sketch the reasons for behaviour, but some authors argue (based usually on the works of Donald Davidson) that it presents causes of it (see, for example, Lennon, 1990).

The philosophical topic of causes and reasons is very complicated, and we must avoid getting lost in the nuances of it. For our purposes, the most important matter is to resist the layman's intuition that for each affair there is a single reason/cause. There are levels of explanation and different kinds of explanation. Moreover, the cause of influenza or schizophrenia, for example, depends on in which causal field it is set (Mackie, 1965). By this, Mackie means that one may approach the question "what causes influenza (or schizophrenia)" in terms of (1) what, statistically speaking, causes the disease, (2) why Tom has got it but not Tim, or (3) why Tom became ill at a certain point in time. The causal field of empirical study consists of humans in general, i.e., it is focused on (1). Psychotherapists' interests reflect the causal fields closer to questions (2) and (3): they focus on the idiosyncratic properties of a person and his or her life history.

It is easy to see that talk about grains of sand and tectonic plates approach matters from different perspectives, and that the former (macro-) perspective is more reasonable when earthquakes are under scrutiny. Similarly, when we present a neuroscientific explanation on a certain act, and an explanation that is couched in terms of commonsense psychology, we should be able to determine the relation between the explanations. However, researchers have been at considerable pains when trying to do that. Bermúdez (2005, pp. 16–39) calls that the *interface problem*.

The problem can be approached through the notion that the terminology of neurosciences, on the one hand, and whatever psychological theory on the other hand, are fundamentally different. The former is said to explain matters on a *subpersonal level*. This means that it is focused on neural or computational mechanisms that perform sub-routines—neuroscientists talk about detections, activations of neurons and neural networks, triggering of neural loops, information-processing algorithms, and so on.

Personal level explanations operate with psychological terms like remembering, thinking, recognizing, feeling, desiring, believing, and knowing. The crucial thing is that the talk about remembering, thinking, and so on makes sense only in the case of (whole) persons—neural structures and thermostats are not entities that could decide something, for example. In their book *Philosophical Foundations of Neuroscience*, Bennett and Hacker (2003, pp. 68–107) show that even leading neuroscientists very often confuse the subpersonal and the personal level, and thus create the *mereological fallacy* by claiming that a certain region of brain, for example, recognized or knew something.

It is extremely illuminating to study psychoanalytic parlance(s) in terms of the above considerations. First, and most importantly, let us note that psychoanalytic talk about unconscious mental matters and commonsense psychology have much in common. As the examples presented previously indicate, psychoanalytic parlance about unconscious matters is part of the commonsense psychology of our times. The significant thing is, however, that, similar to commonsense psychlogy, psychoanalytic third-sphere concepts do not present causes of behaviour in terms of natural sciences, but enable us to reach the reasons or logic behind certain behaviour.

There is no doubt that the explanations of commonsense psychology are often useful, although the terms used in them do not necessarily pinpoint any real entities or processes taking place in one's mind/brain. We should think that this holds—or at least *might* hold—with psychoanalytic explanations using third-sphere concepts, too. The function of both commonsense psychology and psychoanalytic third-sphere parlance is not to state what actually takes place in one's mind/brain in a certain moment, but to enable us to make sense of a person's acts.

If this view of third-sphere concepts is accepted—and I cannot see why it could not be accepted—the questions concerning the essence and existence of the unconscious are not relevant any more. In the next section, I elaborate this view by suggesting that third-sphere concepts should be used in an *instrumentalistic* sense, and seen as *abstracting the functioning of the brain*.

Second, from the perspective of the above considerations, psychoanalytic "faith" in the third-sphere entities appears to be a special case of the mereological fallacy: in psychoanalytic parlance it is very often explicitly or implicitly claimed that a subpersonal-level entity, like censorship, ego, or psychic apparatus, is responsible for acts such as deciding, which only a whole person can perform. Third, the (existence of) interface problems means that sense-making and reason-giving explanations cannot be reduced to the causal explanations of neurosciences, and that implies that it is far from clear how neuropsychoanalysis might help to develop firmer ground for psychoanalysts' work. It is worth stressing here once more that personal and subpersonal explanations are alternatives that approach man from fundamentally different perspectives.

Abstracting the brain—on the "psychoanalytic stance"

In the article "Biting the bullet: the nature of unconscious fantasy" (Talvitie & Ihanus, 2005) we aimed to encroach into the heart of the problems of the three-sphere view. From the perspective of cognitive neuroscience, unconscious fantasy is perhaps the wildest psychoanalytic idea: an outsider cannot even conceive (or fantasize) what kind of entity the psychoanalytic term "unconscious fantasy" might pinpoint. Thus, if one could make clear the logic behind that term from the standpoints of the two-sphere view, there would surely be no problems with repressed desires and fears either. Our heroic effort contains the following fictive example on the psychoanalytic idea of unconscious fantasy:

> Let us suppose that, given an analysand's certain patterns of behavior, an analyst has formulated a hypothesis that the analysand possesses the unconscious fantasy that "My analyst does not respect me, and she may overlook me because of the needs of other analysands and other people." [*ibid.*, p. 672]

The basic issue is that, according to the psychoanalytic view, the mental unconscious also contains unconscious fantasies, but in terms of the two-sphere view, our analyst's hypothesis cannot be made sense of. Let us see how the process of psychotherapy continues.

> One day the analyst gets into a car accident, and so the analysand does not find her analyst when she comes for her analytic session. A fantasy comes to her mind: another patient may be in trouble, and the analyst is seeing him in a psychiatric hospital.

> The fantasy is studied in the next analytic hour, and the analysand talks a lot about her mother and younger sisters: as the oldest child, she had to take care of herself, and her mother concentrated on her younger sisters. She also found a more general notion (fear) in her mind: like her mother, the analyst would probably not pay special attention to her either. Thus, we can make sense of the fantasy from the point of view of the analysand's life history. [ibid., p. 672]

An analyst would hold that the above means that the analyst's hypothesis became verified: the analysand's conscious fantasy matches with the analyst's hypothesis concerning a unconscious fantasy. Since unconscious fantasy is, from the ontological perspective, an oxymoron, that cannot be the case. We can just conclude that the analyst's hypothesis on the unconscious fantasy and the analysand's conscious fantasy have a shared content, and that the analysand's associations concerning her life history fit nicely into the picture. If the hypothesis was of help to the analyst (by enabling her to make useful comments), we must also confess that although there are no such entities as unconscious fantasies, it makes sense to think in terms of them.

Thus, unconscious fantasy is an ontologically flawed, but practically useful presupposition, and on this basis it is plausible to use it in an *instrumentalist sense*.

We determined unconscious fantasy in the spirit of the two-sphere view as follows:

> . . . we should acknowledge that the unconscious processes of the brain affect how we interpret situations (why did the analyst miss the analytic session?), what kind of guesses or suppositions we make (the analyst is meeting another analysand in the hospital), and what kind of conscious fantasies we are disposed to create. Following this kind of thinking, we could say that the analysand possessed preconditions to create a certain kind(s) of fantasy(-ies). "Unconscious fantasy" should be understood as an analyst's hypothesis about what kind of conscious fantasies an analysand is predisposed to produce. [*ibid.*]

We can rephrase the last sentence by stating that the concept "unconscious fantasy" abstracts the functioning of the brain. That formulation can, of course, be applied to unconscious desires, beliefs, and fears as well.

Here we have a reasonable link between neurophysiological processes and psychotherapists' language in general, and between neuroscience and psychoanalysts' third-sphere thinking in particular: behind each phenomenal and behavioural matter there are more or less complex patterns of neural activity, but in psychotherapy it makes no sense to talk about them. Instead, ordinary terms must be used that resonate with the analysand's (and, as well, the analyst's) experiences. When appropriate, therapists' conceptualizations (for example, "Perhaps these matters take place because she has an unconscious fantasy that . . ."; "Maybe you have unconsciously feared . . .") should be held to abstract neural patterns of the brain. We might say that analysts "mentalize" the neural patterns, or "narrate" unconscious neural processes.

Thus, I am proposing that, when thinking and talking in terms of the third-sphere concepts, psychoanalysts should not be seen to be referring to real entities, but to be using those concepts instrumentally, in the service of the aims of therapy. This is attitude (B), as presented in Chapter Three: third-sphere concepts should be seen as theoretical ones.

Considering the topics and arguments of the previous chapters, a reader may hold that I have created a cheap *ad hoc* solution to the confusions presented at the beginning of the chapter: unconscious desires, fantasies, and fears do not exist, but psychoanalysts may carry on talking about them as they have done for a century. One might also remark that the view I am advocating illustrates the mereological fallacy in an excellent manner.

My solution is not cheap or artificial, however. First, for the psychoanalytic folk a turn from the "realistic" conception of the third-sphere concepts to an instrumentalist one is not a minor change—let us remind ourselves that we are dealing with the "cornerstone". Second, my approach does not blindly legitimate all psychoanalytic parlance: it deals with only the third-sphere concepts, and an instrumentalist use of the concepts is legitimate *only if* it supports the aims of psychotherapy (this is an empirical issue); like hypotheses in general, psychoanalysts' hypotheses on unconscious fantasies, for example, may lack support. Third, my solution reflects the state of things with psychological concepts in general, and it is also a strategy that Daniel Dennett has been systemically developing in the domain of cognitive science.

Let us think of the psychological concepts "schemata" and "coping mechanism". Researchers are not able to identify the neural correlates for a "restaurant scheme", or a certain coping mechanism. Instead, psychological concepts address behavioural patterns that are of interest in terms of explaining behaviour and making sense of humans' acts and reactions. Thus, the instrumentalist use of the third-sphere concepts would reflect the general state of things in the domain of psychology.

The philosopher Daniel Dennett has created a model on the relations between different kinds of explanations (see Dennett, 1978, pp. 3–22, 1987, pp. 13–35), and he often stresses the need to abstract complex dynamics of the brain. According to him, there are two reasons for abstracting neurophysiological matters. First, often we simply do not know the neurophysiological details. Second, in many cases neurophysiological explanations were too long and complicated, and as such would not serve the interest of a researcher.

The need to abstract physical reality is not restricted to humans as objects of study, and not even to living organisms. When studying this issue or that concerning the levels of explanation, Dennett often uses a computer as an example. Let us follow him and turn to think of the functioning of computers.

Computers are man-made machines, and there are no mysteries about how they work—in principle, a complete explanation of a computer's functioning is always at hand. However, often—or, indeed, mainly—it is not reasonable to explain the "behaviour" of a computer in terms of what happens in its hardware. Such explanations were extremely long and complicated, and in most cases they were also irrelevant, considering one's interests. Let us think of a humanist learning to use a computer. He wonders why a certain icon appears on the screen every time the computer is turned on. It is clear that a story on what happens in the hardware (a *physical level explanation* in Dennett's terminology) would not be helpful, and thus a friendly nerd (or computer engineer) tells another story:

> It is an icon of an anti-virus programme. Electronic viruses spread through the internet, and those programmes could be seen as electronic defence mechanisms. Computers *aim to* protect themselves from the viruses, and, by flashing the icon, the computer just *wants to tell* you that the anti-virus programme is *awake*.

The nerd abstracts the functioning of the computer by projecting intentional and phenomenal states ("aim to", "wants to tell", "awake") into a computer. Dennett holds that such an explanatory strategy—projecting intentional states into organisms—is legitimate and useful when it is employed to make sense of, for example, behavioural patterns having emerged in the course of evolution ("... tries to spread his genes as effectively as possible ..."). One might characterize Dennett's model by stating that, after having become very, very conscious of the mereological fallacy (and homunculus fallacy), one may use it as an explanatory strategy.

When psychoanalysts' thinking is conceptualized in terms of the two-sphere view, Dennett's idea strikes home: analysts aim to make sense of the analysands' acts and reactions by projecting intentional states into persons' unconscious mind/brain, which means abstracting the complicated dynamics of the brain. Robert Rushing (2006, pp. 192–194) calls this *psychoanalytic stance*. (In Talvitie [2003], I present my Freudo-Dennettian approach in a more detailed manner. See also Talvitie & Ihanus [2005].)

Repression, for example, can be explained on different levels of abstraction. When a person represses a feeling of envy in a certain situation we can, first, tell the neurophysiological story on a neural level: in Tim's brain the neuron N^1 fires in a frequency 4, the neuron N^2 fires in a frequency 9, the neuron N^3 fires in a frequency of 7, and so on. Second, we can describe the neural activity on the level of networks, detections, and population codes. Third, we can state "A non-attended feeling of envy was detected by the brain, which triggered neural algorithms that made Tim think of Tom's problems with alcohol". Fourth, we can set the event in a larger context. Above, the nerd approached certain processes of the computer in terms of their (defensive) function, and similarly we can state "Tim—or, actually, neural apparatus of his brain—repressed his feeling of envy in order to protect his narrative self".

A further look inside computers serves as a lead to the topic of different explanatory levels studied after the next section: when there are problems with a computer, one possibility is that its electronic circuits are damaged. This possibility is equivalent to neurophysiological damage in humans. The other possibility concerns programmes and their interaction. In that case, the hardware is intact, and a computer engineer directs her intervention to the programmes by updating them, for instance. Similarly, the most reasonable explanations for human behaviour are far from always neurophysiological, and a useful intervention to psychic/existential problems (a technique of psychotherapy) need not necessarily even be formulated in neurophysiological terms.

Darwin, Freud, and the illusion of the hidden designer

When processes and characteristics fit too well into a big picture, and appear as necessary components of a complex, apparently goal-directed system, an illusion emerges: we are tempted to think that those processes and characteristics are designed by a human-like agent. At the beginning of this book we studied that illusion in the case of oddities of behaviour: previously, oddities have been approached in terms of supernatural explanations, i.e., they were thought to be caused by gods and evil forces. The development of psychology in general, and both psychoanalytic and cognitive views on the unconscious in particular, have led to a demystification of the oddities.

That illusion is also the focus of Charles Darwin's work. In pre-Darwinian times the processes taking place in nature, and in the traits of animals and plants, were seen as designed by God (and one can still hear talk about an "intelligent designer"). Darwin revealed the connection between the prevalence of traits and behavioural dispositions on the one hand, and the survival of a species on the other. Evolutionary theory demystifies the illusion of the human-like agent by showing how the logic of evolution supports the emergence of traits and behavioural dispositions that are "useful" in the life of an organism. It is talked about as evolutionary functions of traits and behavioural dispositions.

The problems with the third-sphere view can also be seen from the above perspective: Freud revealed that slips, dreams, and disorders are not accidental or random phenomena, but are connected to the desires, fears, and the life history of the person in question—those phenomena appeared to be serving a purpose of some kind, or being "designed" somehow. The illusion on purposes was impressive, and that led Freud to project into the mind rather human-like agencies (id, ego, superego, censorship, psychic apparatus). Closely related to that, the illusion also led him to presuppose a sphere—the unconscious part of the mind—in which dynamics would give rise to slips, dreams, and disorders: the meaning or purpose of those phenomena could be tracked to the unconscious. Thus, it is appropriate to claim that Freudian theory contains an implicit idea that the mental unconscious is an unobservable designer of such phenomena.

Evolutionary theory was very important to Freud (see Sulloway, 1979), and Ernest Jones (1913, p. xii) even called him the "Darwin of the mind". In Freud's times, however, even the superiority of Darwin's model over Lamarck's was not yet clear, and the larger significance of Darwin's thinking was revealed only in the second half of the twentieth century. In the 1950s and 1960s, philosophers of science such as Carl Gustav Hempel and Ernst Nagel took on the role of functional explanations in science under scrutiny (McLaughlin, 2001, pp. 63–137; Salmon, 1989, pp. 26–32), and it was only in the 1970s that the essence of functions were focused on by the philosophers of biology (Cummins [1975], and Wright [1973] being the classic articles). Thus, it is not a surprise that Freud did not apply the logic of evolutionary thinking in a more profound manner.

What is surprising is that even the classics of biological psychoanalysis (Badcock, 1994; Kandel, 2005; Slavin & Kriegman, 1992) do not make the connection that the logic of evolutionary theory could be applied to psychoanalysis. Only occasionally (Braddock, 2006; Manson, 2003; Talvitie & Ihanus, 2006) is the idea brought forward that "explanation in psychoanalytic psychology is functional in the same way as functional explanation in the life sciences such as biology and behavioural science . . ." (Braddock, 2006, p. 402).

Functions are at the core of both evolutionary theory and psychoanalysis: Darwin revealed the evolutionary functions of the traits of species, and Freud the repressive functions of ideas, disorders, and acts. The above considerations give us good reason to think that, if applied in a profound manner, evolutionary theory would resolve the problem of the hidden designer.

According to three-sphere view thinking, there are three ontological levels, and corresponding levels of explanation: behaviour is explained by referring to conscious mental states, unconscious mental states, or brain states. Although the two-sphere view of cognitive neuroscience presupposes just two *ontological* levels (conscious and brain states), three *explanatory* levels are applied in the scope of it. The middle level explanations—called *design stance* by Dennett—consist of functional explanations. The moral of the story below will be that the third-sphere concepts used by psychoanalysts should not be seen from the ontological perspective, i.e., whether or not they refer to existing entities. Instead, they should be seen as forming design-level explanations.

Intentional, physical, and design-level explanations

Daniel Dennett developed a model on different levels of explanation based on Marr (1982). In his system, explanatory levels are *stances*. The term implies that there is no fixed connection between the phenomenon under scrutiny, and certain level of explanation. Instead, the latter depends on *how* the researcher is interested in the phenomenon.

Intentional stance explanations refer to desires, fears, beliefs, and motives of a "system". Intentional stance thinking characterizes commonsense psychology. In his model, Dennett admits the strength of commonsense psychology and suggests that it is plausible to apply intentional stance in a technical manner to every kind of system—intentional stance approach may be applied regardless if the "system" actually possesses phenomenal states. That idea was illustrated in the above example on the nerd lecturing a humanist on the aims and desires of a computer. I also claimed that psychoanalysts' talk about third-sphere concepts should be seen as reflecting an intentional stance (or "psychoanalytic stance"): desires, fears, and so on are projected to the system unconscious, which actually is just a neurophysiological system.

Physical stance means simply neurophysiological explanations. In the post-Freudian era this level was for decades (mainly) held as useless for psychoanalysts. Along with neuropsychoanalysis, the pendulum has swung to the opposite end: there are attempts to anchor even Freud's metapsychological ideas and the effectiveness of psychotherapy to neurophysiological matters.

It is reasonable to illustrate *design stance* through evolutionary explanations. (For further reading on evolutionary explanations and functions, see Ariew, Cummins, & Perlman [2002]; Mayr [1997, pp. 112–119]; McLaughlin [2001].)

In the scope of physical stance, the question "Why do giraffes have long necks?" is to be answered with "Due to the gene X". The answer is a true one, but it does not necessarily satisfy one's curiosity. The design stance answer, "Because it renders it possible to reach leaves—which a giraffe eats—from the tops of the trees", refers to the *function* of the neck, and is true as well. The claim that a certain characteristic possesses a function can be justified from two perspectives. First, *historically* (this perspective originates from Hempel's and Wright's writings): the necks of earlier giraffes became gradually longer because long necks increased the fitness of a giraffe—long-necked giraffes survived better, and thus also gave birth to a greater number of descendants. Thus, it is legitimate and reasonable to claim that the function of giraffes' necks is to render it possible to reach leaves from the tops of trees.

Another way to justify the concept function is *systemic* (Nagel and Cummins laid the ground for that perspective): each organism is a system consisting of many traits, properties, organs, and sub-systems, and these parts (or sub-systems) are interdependent. The usefulness of the long necks of present-day giraffes depends on their other traits or properties—if giraffes were carnivores living in the jungle, long necks would probably be of no use. Similarly, the function of heart (to pump blood) is tied to the existence and functions of blood-vessels, lungs, and so on. Thus, also from the systemic perspective, it is reasonable and legitimate to hold that the function of a long neck is to render it possible to reach leaves from the tops of trees.

Through this kind of logic, evolutionary theory explains the properties that "fit too well to the big picture", and demystifies the idea of hidden designer. A psychoanalytically orientated reader can easily approach Dennett's system through the lens of the three-sphere view, and confuse ontological levels with the levels of explanation (for example, Solms, 2006; Žižek, 2006, p. 237). Thus, let us emphasize that *nothing exists on the design level*. It would be absurd to state that the function of giraffe's long neck existed there. There are, however, concepts that characterize design-level explanations—that of function, in particular. Design stance is just another way to approach certain "why" questions, and design-level explanations do not compete with neurophysiological causal ones.

The functions and history of a system are at the core of design-level explanations. Since Robert Cummins' *The Nature of Psychological Explanation* (Cummins, 1983) the concept function has also characterized psychological explanations (Bermúdez, 2005, pp. 52–70; Feest, 2003; Looren de Jong, 2003). The nature of psychological explanations is often presented through the computer metaphor: a psychologist is not interested in the hardware (brain) but the pro-grammes, and the functions of those programmes. Psychoanalysts, too, are familiar with functions. First, they think all the time of the defensive functions of analysands' acts, behavioural dispositions, attitudes, and so on. Second, in Freud's metapsychology, the concept function enjoys a key role: the function of whatever act is to decrease psychic tension.

On the above basis it is clear that, regardless of whether one "believes in" the third sphere, we need three distinct explanatory levels when studying humans. Below, psychoanalytic thinking is set in the Denettian framework. To put it in a nutshell, I will suggest that, similar to the way in which evolutionary biology studies physical traits and behavioural dispositions of *species* from the historical and functionalistic perspective, psychoanalysis studies psychical traits and behavioural dispositions of an *individual* from historical and functionalistic perspective.

Psychoanalysis and the levels of explanation

In psychoanalysis, analysands' ideas (contents of consciousness), psychic defects, general proclivities to interpret matters in a certain way (for example, in a paranoid, passive, submissive, masochistic, or hopeless manner) and more specific proclivities like losing control in certain situations, and forming relationships accompanied by violence, are studied. People go to psychotherapy when they cannot manage their problems by using commonsense psychology.

The problems do possess neural counterparts of some kind, and neuropsychiatry approaches the problems in terms of physical stance by trying to find effective drugs. Psychoanalytic therapy tries to change the problematic matters by making sense of them. As we will see, that aim falls within the scope of design stance.

In terms of design stance, the sense-making aim of psychoanalysis means that it attempts to find the functions of those problematic matters, which also means that it attempts to put them in context. Following the two ways to determine functions presented above, there are two contexts: historical and systemic. Psychoanalysis is known for emphasizing the significance of early years of development, and putting matters into the *historical context* means simply that current matters are connected to an analysand's earlier experiences and conditions of life.

Let us think of woman who becomes absent-minded every time she hears a man talking in an aggressive manner. In terms of physical stance, the reaction is to be approached from the viewpoint that the "stimulus" of a man's aggressive tone triggers neural processes that cause absent-mindedness. In psychotherapy, the woman's reaction was studied from the historical perspective: her father was an alcoholic who was aggressive when drunk. That was very distressing for a small girl, and she learned to cope with it by becoming absent-minded when necessary. At first, the girl used that defence consciously, but later it "turned on" automatically. Thus, the woman and the analyst found the function of the reaction: to avoid distress. Due to the working through that took place in psychotherapy, the woman remembered more clearly her early years, but she also became conscious of the function of her reaction.

Paul Skokowski (2003) has suggested that when we are able to put neural processes (or structures) triggering such reactions in a historical context this way, it is plausible to talk about implicit beliefs. Following Skokowski's line of thought, the historical context would legitimate the talk about implicit (or unconscious) desires and fears as well. This kind definition of beliefs does not presume that beliefs and desires are somehow mental.

Let us spell out the similarity between evolutionary explanations and the one above. The "why" questions, "Why are giraffes necks long?", and "Why does the woman become absent-minded when hearing a man talk aggressively", can be given answers in terms of physical stance ("due to gene X"; "due to neural patterns of Z and Y"). However, the disciplines of evolutionary biology and psychoanalysis are interested in different "whys"—long necks and a woman's reaction can be made sense of by focusing on the historical conditions that gave rise to them.

In the case of humans' minds and psychotherapy, the *systemic context* means the whole of the ideas, desires, fears, and so on that one possesses—i.e., the narrative self. Let us think of a man who always remembers to mention the shortness of his successful colleague. The colleague has several traits—shortness and brilliant intellect among them—and by focusing on the height, the superior intellect remains on the background. Consequently, also the fact that our man is less intelligent than the shorter colleague remains marginal. Thus, it is plausible to claim that, in terms of the systemic context (of the narrative self), focusing on the height possesses the function of avoiding a feeling of jealousy.

Let us highlight again the similarity of an evolutionary explanation (or, in this case, rather a *biological* explanation) and our example. In terms of the systemic definition, the function of a trait, tendency, behavioural disposition, or property depends on its role in the system—the function of the heart depends on other organs, and we should be able to see the behavioural disposition of blaming that way, too. As presented in the previous chapter, the narrative self should be seen as a system, and our man's view of himself as an intelligent person and skilful professional is one part of his narrative self. In order to keep systemic definition apart from the historical one, let us stress that for whatever reason the man focuses on his colleague's height, the factual effect of it is that he is less envious and regards himself as a more intelligent and more skilful professional. On this basis it is legitimate to claim that the behavioural disposition possessed a function of repressing the feeling of envy and protecting the narrative self.

The biologist Ernst Mayr introduced the distinction between ultimate (or remote) and proximate reasons (see Ariew, 2003). An explanation seeking ultimate reasons refers to the evolutionary origins of a trait or a behavioural disposition, whereas proximate reasons pinpoint an organism's mechanisms and physiological structures—genes, for example. Fred Dretske (2004) modifies Mayr's distinction by talking about *triggering* and *structural causes*. Dretske illustrates his distinction through the following example.

> A terrorist plants a bomb in the general's car. The bomb sits there for days until the general gets in his car and turns the key to start the engine. The bomb is detonated (triggered by turning the key in the ignition) and the general is killed. Who killed him? The terrorist, of course. How? By planting a bomb in his car. Although the general's own action (turning on the engine) was the triggering cause, the terrorist's action, wiring the bomb to the ignition, is the structuring cause, and it will surely be the terrorist's action, something that happened a week ago, that will be singled out, in both legal and moral inquiries, as the cause of the explosion that resulted in the general's death. [*ibid.*, p. 169]

Triggering cause refers to the here-and-now conditions, whereas structural cause tells the there-and-then reasons why the process is the way it is. The above example shows that triggering causes are often coincidental: the terrorist connected the bomb to the ignition, but the trigger might have been the steering wheel or the door as well. Similarly, in my computer, the key F1 starts up the Cubase programme, but the trigger might equally well be F4 or F8. The crucial thing is that in order to make the use of the computer more fluent, someone (actually, it was myself) set the structural cause by programming the function keys in a certain way.

Dretske's distinction enables us to formulate the characteristics of psychoanalytic praxis from the viewpoint of cognitive orientation. That is, matters such as anguish, compulsive behaviour, absent-mindedness, snake phobia, and bulimic behaviour also have both triggering and structural causes. The triggering cause should be held to refer both to a certain stimulus (comparable to the keys of the general's car and my computer) and the neural processes it triggers in the brain. In behavioural therapy, snake phobia is approached through the triggering cause: the person is desensitized to snakes, the triggering stimulus. Similarly, when ordering drugs, psychiatrists think of neural processes that give rise to disorders—i.e., here-and-now triggering causes.

In contrast to psychiatrists and behavioural therapists, psychoanalysts are interested in the structuring causes. They try to reach how the analysand's brain has become structured (or "designed") in such a way that certain matters trigger anxiety, bulimic behaviour, absent-mindedness, and so on. The behavioural dispositions of species are designed in the course of evolutionary history, and the structural causes of computers are set by computer engineers (or programmers). Idiosyncratic behavioural dispositions have been designed in the course of one's personal life history, in a manner that the above example of the absent-minded woman and countless psychoanalytic case studies illustrate. Thus, we can rephrase the common knowledge that psychoanalysts are interested in childhood by stating that they possess a specific interest in how the triggering causes have become formed. As we see, the concepts' structural cause, "historical context" and "function" (when determined historically), refer to the same matters.

When psychotherapeutic sense-making causes a disorder to disappear, it means that a triggering cause has also changed—psychotherapy has changed the brain. In the article "The repressed and implicit knowledge (Talvitie & Ihanus, 2002), we proposed a model on that. In a nutshell, our model goes as follows: it is the system of implicit knowledge (unconscious detections and neural algorithms) that gives rise to disorders. When a disorder vanishes, it means that the functioning of that system has changed in one way or another. In psychoanalysis, one gains insight on the functions and structural causes of disorders, and that knowledge is represented in the system of explicit knowledge. We should think that, in the post-therapy situation, either the functioning of the implicit knowledge system has altered, or neural structures of explicit knowledge are able to inhibit it.

In order to see that the intentional, physical, and design-level explanations are complementary and non-contradictory, and that the appropriate level of explanations depends on one's interests, let us think of Pam, who intends to interrupt her psychotherapy because she thinks that her analyst is rude. Whether or not Pam's claim has grounds, it has to be taken seriously: her idea of interrupting therapy is connected to that claim, and it must not be overlooked as just a defensive, commonsense psychology statement. We should approach Pam's claim as an intentional stance explanation: the therapist's rudeness makes her feel bad, and that causes her to interrupt therapy.

Pam's claim surely has neural correlates, and thus it is possible to present—at least in principle—a physical stance explanation for her desire to interrupt therapy. However, a psychoanalyst's job is to approach the matters taking place in psychotherapy in terms of the design stance. Thus, she thinks of the possible functions and structural reasons for wanting to interrupt psychotherapy: perhaps Pam has been used to escape from close relationships by breaking them (historical context, structural causes); perhaps Pam fears that the topics that she has lately talked about will make the therapist abandon her (systemic context).

Pam's aim may be approached in terms of each stance. The therapist may present an interpretation that arises from her design stance thinking, or she may turn to Pam's commonsense (psychology) by saying that the idea of ending the relationship often arises in psychotherapy, and that it has to be studied just in the same way as other ideas. If Pam's suspicion towards her analyst is paranoid in essence, it is possible that drugs—the physical stance intervention—would be of help.

Let us still make a point on the relation between design-level explanation and intentional stance as applied by psychoanalysts (a "psychoanalytic stance" explanation). A certain phenomenon may be explained by claiming "the function of Jane's absent-mindedness is to protect her from distressing memories and foreseeable ideas concerning male aggressiveness" (design stance explanation) or "Jane possesses an unconscious fear of male aggressiveness" (intentional/psychoanalytic stance explanation). It is easy to see that the psychoanalytic stance claim is just a version of the design stance claim, and practical reasons determine which one should be favoured.

*   *   *

For a psychoanalytically orientated reader the above considerations sound familiar. In the scope of psychoanalysis it has been used to talk about repressive functions of different matters, and the term "historical context" refers to matters that have been called *genetic (historical) explanation*, while "systemic context" has been called *psychodynamics*. However, mirroring carefully the design stance thinking of evolutionary biology has important consequences.

If we consider the core elements of psychoanalytic psychotherapy in terms of the three-sphere view, it can make sense only from the psychoanalytic viewpoint. However, if the third *ontological* level is given up, and the clinical practice of psychoanalysis is approached through (the four-level model and) the *explanatory level* of design stance, tensions between psychoanalysis and present-day behavioural sciences are relieved. It is difficult to overestimate the significance of that matter for the future of psychoanalysis.

Epilogue: history of the future of psychoanalysis

The Finnish composer Eero Hämeenniemi has written a fascinating book, the title of which in English is "The History of the Music of the Future" (Hämeenniemi, 2007). The name is not just a hilarious joke. Hämeenniemi studies the current and coming status of classical music, and makes the common connection that it is strongly anchored to past heroes, rituals, and conventions—orchestras play 200-year-old compositions wearing costumes that were in fashion decades ago, and the audience is supposed to passively receive the creation. Classical music is in crisis—respect of tradition has made it lose contact with the surrounding world.

The history of present-day psychoanalysis is usually written by focusing on the first half of the twentieth century—i.e., by referring (mainly) to Sigmund Freud's ground-breaking studies. The crisis of psychoanalysis resembles that of classical music: if psychoanalysis continues to lean on Freud's works for another hundred years, its credibility will probably vanish completely. Hämeenniemi reminds us that the future of classical music depends on what takes place in the scope of classical music today. Similarly, we must think that at the moment we are living the history of the future of psychoanalysis—the future of psychoanalysis is created *now*.

Hämeenniemi approaches classical music by focusing on the relations between a composer, musicians, and the audience. In contrast to the many other music genres, the musicians follow composers' ideas rather faithfully. Both composers and musicians have a rather formal relation to the audience: composers—if alive— do not necessarily play in public, and the audience is advised to "behave"—not to disturb the musicians. All in all, Hämeenniemi argues that the relations between the corners are not *vivacious*.

Hämeenniemi's triangle can be applied to psychoanalysis by replacing the audience with patients, musicians with psychoanalysts, and composers/compositions with psychoanalytic theory. Psychoanalysts' work could be seen as continual improvisation that is based on psychoanalytic theory and takes place in a clinical situation. When it comes to the vivacity of this psychoanalytic triangle, we can make the general assumption that the relations between therapists and patients are usually vivacious, and that patients do not necessarily need to know their therapists' background theory. The lack of vivacity concerns the corner of theory, and the problems with that corner can be stated as follows.

In this book I have focused on the unconscious, but psychoanalytic models contradict present-day views in many other respects, too. In addition to this *interdisciplinary* tension, psychoanalytic models also have *intradisciplinary* ones: there have been disputes between Freudians, Lacanians, Kleinians, ego-psychoanalysis, and so on. In the domain of science, evidence becomes cumulated sooner or later in favour of one of the rival hypotheses. These psychoanalytic disputes, however, seem to be immune to clinical and empirical evidence—neither shared clinical data of psychoanalysts nor empirical studies have verified or falsified competing hypotheses.

In the domain of physics, fundamental changes took place during a period of about ten years at the turn of the nineteenth and twentieth centuries: X-rays, the electron, and radioactivity were revealed, and discoveries on quantum action and relativity theory were made by Planck and Einstein. Before that, the community of physicists lived in a undisturbed world—in 1894 the physicist Albert Michaelson said,

> ... it seems probable that most of the grand underlying principles have been firmly established and that further advances are to be

sought chiefly in the rigorous application of the principles to all the phenomena which come under our notice. [cited in Kragh, 1999, p. 3]

Michaelson's statement represents the attitude of many present-day psychoanalysts: it is believed that Freud/Lacan/Klein got it mainly right (". . . most of the grand underlying principles have been firmly established . . .") and that the theory needs just be slightly amended and applied to current topics (". . . further advances are to be sought chiefly in the rigorous application of the principles to all the phenomena which come under our notice").

For the future of psychoanalysis such an attitude is the kiss of death: psychoanalytic thinking needs an urgent and profound update, since it contradicts present-day views of science in numerous respects. Many hold that psychoanalysis is simply outdated. But how is it possible that psychoanalytic theory has—similarly to classical music—lost its contact to the surrounding world in such a fundamental manner?

A psychoanalyst works outside the scientific community, and, after having obtained a licence, has no compelling reason to care about psychoanalytic communities either. Thus, a psychoanalyst's economical success is dependent only on the patients, and—in contrast to the scientists—he or she is not forced to take seriously views that challenge his or her models.

Chapter Three made it clear that the stagnant attitude also concerns neuropsychoanalysis, the most modern branch of psychoanalysis: ontological considerations, among others, are passed, and cognitive neuroscience is supposed just to provide the final proof for certain Freudian presuppositions. All in all, present-day psychoanalytic thinking is (mainly) conservative, and the psychoanalytic community is (mainly) reluctant to take an unprejudiced look at its foundations, and thus also unable to apply non-psychoanalytic research in an open-minded manner. If the future of psychoanalysis is dark, the reason lies in the history sketched above.

Psychoanalysis is not, however, doomed to such a dark future. It is not less scientific than other psychotherapies, and it has always resonated with a wide range of topics from neuroscientific issues to film theory—in a word, psychoanalysis has potential.

Hämeenniemi's idea behind the word-play is that we should consider our present acts and attitudes in terms of what kind of future they imply. When this book is studied as a (piece of) history of future psychoanalysis, individual claims, arguments, and models are meaningless. The crucial thing is—I think—the general aim of setting the "psychoanalytic" issues in the context of present-day views. I have not tried to be "modern" by using concepts that are brand new—at least when compared with the psychoanalytic ones. Instead, I have aimed at create a lively contact between psycho-analysis and cognitive neuroscience. I hope that the reader also has a lively contact with this book—which means objections, and insights not shared by the author, among other things.

We should resist thinking that terms like population code, neural loop, interface problem, design-level explanation, mereolog-ical fallacy, and triggering cause reflect "true and reasonable scien-tific thought", which psychoanalysis should incorporate. Instead, these terms represent efforts that have been made in order to solve certain problems of behavioural sciences. In the current state of things, psychoanalytic folk use psychoanalytic terms and, not surprisingly, there seem also to be specific psychoanalytic prob-lems. I hope that future theories of psychoanalysis will, for the most part, share both concepts and problems with other branches of behavioural science.

REFERENCES

Allen, J. G., & Fonagy, P. (Eds.) (2006). *The Handbook of Mentalization-Based Treatment*. Chichester: Wiley.

Ariew, A. (2003). Ernst Mayr's "ultimate /proximate" distinction reconsidered and reconstructed. *Biology and Philosophy, 18*: 553–565.

Ariew, A., Cummins, R., & Perlman, M. (Eds.) (2002). *Functions: New Essays in the Philosophy of Psychology and Biology*. Oxford: Oxford University Press.

Baars, B. (1997). *In the Theatre of Consciousness*. New York: Oxford University Press.

Badcock, C. (1994). *PsychoDarwinism: The New Synthesis of Darwin and Freud*. London: HarperCollins.

Baker, L. R. (2003). Belief ascription and the illusion of depth. *Facta Philosophica, 5*: 183–201.

Bargh, J. A. (1990). Auto-motives: preconscious determinants of social interaction. In: E. T. Higgins & R. M. Sorrentino (Eds.), *Handbook of Motivation and Cognition: Foundations of Social Behavior* (Vol. 2, pp. 93–130). New York: Guilford.

Bennett, M. R., & Hacker, P. M. S. (2003). *Philosophical Foundations of Neuroscience*. Malden, MA: Blackwell.

Bermúdez, J. L. (2005). *Philosophy of Psychology: A Contemporary Introduction*. New York: Routledge.

Berry, D. C. (1997). Introduction. In: D. C. Berry (Ed.), *How Implicit is Implicit Learning?* (pp. 1–12). Oxford: Oxford University Press.

Bettelheim, B. (1982). *Freud and Man's Soul*. London: Flamingo.

Bonioli, G. (2000). What does it mean to observe physical reality? In: Agazzi & M. Pauri (Eds.), *The Reality of the Unobservable* (pp. 177–190). Dordrecht: Kluwer Academic Publishers.

Bornstein, R. F. (1990). Subliminal mere exposure and psychodynamic activation effects: implications for the psychoanalytic theory of conscious and unconscious mental processes. In: J. Masling (Ed.), *Empirical Studies of Psychoanalytic Theories*, Vol. III (pp. 55–88). Hillsdale, NJ: Erlbaum.

Bouveresse, J. (1991). *Wittgenstein Reads Freud: The Myth of the Unconscious*. C. Cosman (Trans.). Princeton, NJ: Princeton University Press.

Braddock, L. E. (2006). Psychoanalysis as functionalist social science: the legacy of Freud's "Project for a scientific psychology". *Studies in History and Philosophy of Biological and Biomedical Sciences*, 37: 394–413.

Brakel, L. (2003). Commentary on "On the nature of repressed contents". *Neuro-Psychoanalysis*, 5(2): 142–146.

Broad, C. D. (1975). *Leibniz: An Introduction*. London: Cambridge University Press.

Canguilhem, G. (1994). *A Vital Rationalist: Selected Writings from Georges Canguilhem*. A. Goldhammer (Trans.). New York: Zone Books.

Chalmers, D. J. (1996). *The Conscious Mind: In Search of a Fundamental Theory*. Oxford: Oxford University Press.

Channell, D. F. (1991). *The Vital Machine: A Study of Technology and Organic Life*. New York: Oxford University Press.

Chartrand, T. L., & Bargh, J. A. (1996). Automatic activation of social information processing goals: nonconscious priming reproduces effects of explicit conscious instructions. *Journal of Personality and Social Psychology*, 71: 464–478.

Chartrand, T. L., & Bargh, J. A. (2002). Nonconscious motivations: their activation, operation, and consequences. In: A. Tesser, D. A. Stapel, & J. V. Wood (Eds.), *Self and Motivation: Emerging Psychological Perspectives* (pp. 13–41). Washington, DC: American Psychological Association.

Churchland, P. (1996). *The Engine of Reason, The Seat of Soul*. Cambridge, MA: MIT Press.

Churchland, P. S. (2002). *BRAIN-WISE: Studies in Neurophilosophy*. Cambridge, MA: MIT Press.

Claxton, G. (2005). *The Wayward Mind: An Intimate History of The Unconscious.* London: Little, Brown.

Cohen, R. (2005). *The Record Men: Chess Records and The Birth of Rock & Roll.* London: Profile.

Colby, K. M. (1981). Modeling a paranoid mind. *Behavioral and Brain Sciences, 4*: 515–560.

Colby, K. M., & Stoller, R. J. (1988). *Cognitive Science and Psychoanalysis.* Hillsdale, NJ: Analytic Press.

Colman, A. M. (2001). *Oxford Dictionary of Psychology.* Oxford: Oxford University Press.

Copleston, F. (1958). *The Rationalists: Descartes to Leibnitz. History of Philosophy, Vol. 4.* London: Continuum.

Copleston, F. (1963). *18th and 19th century German Philosophy. History of Philosophy, Vol. 7.* London: Continuum.

Cottingham, J. (1992). Cartesian dualism: theology, metaphysics, and science. In: J. Cottingham (Ed.), *The Cambridge Companion to Descartes* (pp. 236–257). Cambridge: Cambridge University Press.

Cranefield, P. F. (1966a). The philosophical and cultural interests of the biophysics movement of 1847. *Journal of the History of Medicine and Allied Sciences, 21*: 1–7.

Cranefield, P. F. (1966b). Freud and the "School of Helmholtz". *Gesnerius, 23*: 35–39.

Csikszentmihalyi, M. (1990). *Flow: The Psychology of Optimal Experience.* New York: Harper & Row.

Cummins, R. (1975). Functional analysis. *Journal of Philosophy, 72*: 741–764.

Cummins, R. (1983). *The Nature of Psychological Explanation.* Cambridge, MA: MIT Press.

Davis, M. (2000). *The Universal Computer: The Road from Leibniz to Turing.* New York: W. W. Norton.

de Gelder, B., de Haan, E., & Heywood, C. (2001). Introduction. In: B. de Gelder, E. de Haan, & C. Heywood (Eds.), *Out of Mind: Varieties of Unconscious Processes* (pp. ix–xvi). Oxford: Oxford University Press.

Dennett, D. (1989). The origins of selves. *Cogito, 3*: 163–173.

Dennett, D. (1991). *Consciousness Explained.* Boston, MA: Little, Brown.

Dennett, D. C. (1978). *Brainstorms: Philosophical Essays on Mind and Psychology.* London: Penguin.

Dennett, D. C. (1987). *Intentional Stance.* Cambridge, MA: The MIT Press.

Dennett, D. C. (2003). *Freedom Evolves.* London: Penguin.

Dennett, D. C., & Haugeland, J. (1998). Intentionality. In: R. L. Gregory (Ed.), *The Oxford Companion to the Mind* (pp. 383–386). Oxford: Oxford University Press.

Dennett, D., & Humphrey, N. (1989). Speaking for ourselves. *Raritan: A Quarterly Review*, 1: 68–98. Reprinted in D. Dennett (1998), *Brainchildren: Essays on Designing Minds* (pp. 31–55). London: Penguin.

Dretske, F. (1995). *Naturalizing the Mind*. Cambridge, MA: MIT Press.

Dretske, F. (2004). Psychological vs. biological explanations of behavior. *Behavior and Philosophy*, 32: 167–177.

Dreyfus, H. L. (1972). *What Computers Can't Do: A Critique of Artificial Reason*. New York: Harper & Row.

Drinka, G. F. (1984). *The Birth of Neurosis: Myth, Malady and the Victorians*. New York: Simon and Schuster.

Edelman, G. M., & Tononi, G. (2000). *Consciousness: How Matter Becomes Imagination*. London: Penguin.

Edmonds, D., & Eidinow, J. (2001). *Wittgenstein's Poker: The Story of a Ten-Minute Argument between two Great Philosophers*. Chatham: Faber and Faber.

Edwards, D., & Jacobs, M (2003). *Conscious and Unconscious*. Berkshire: Open University Press.

Ellenberger, H. F. (1970). *The Discovery of the Unconscious: The History and Evolution of Dynamic Psychiatry*. London: Fontana.

Erdelyi, M. H. (1996). *The Recovery of the Unconscious Memories: Hypermnesia and Reminiscence*. Chicago, IL: University of Chicago Press.

Feest, U. (2003). Functional analysis and the autonomy of psychology. *Philosophy of Science*, 70: 937–948.

Fichtner, G. (Ed.) (1992). *The Sigmund Freud–Ludwig Binswanger Correspondence 1909–1938*. New York: Other Press.

Fodor, J. (1983). *Modularity of Mind: An Essay on Faculty Psychology*. Cambridge, MA: MIT Press.

Freud, S. (1895). *Project for a Scientific Psychology. S.E.*, 1: 283–398. London: Hogarth.

Freud, S. (1905c). *Jokes and Their Relation to the Unconscious. S.E.*, 8. London Hogarth.

Freud, S. (1915e). *Das Unbewusste. Gesammelte Werke*, 10: 264–303.

Freud, S. (1915e). The unconscious. *S.E.*, 14: 166–204. London: Hogarth.

Freud, S. (1916–1917). *Introductory Lectures on Psycho-Analysis. S.E.*, 15–16. London: Hogarth.

Freud, S. (1923b). *The Ego and the Id. S.E.*, 19: 3–66. London: Hogarth.

Freud, S. (1940a). *An Outline of Psycho-Analysis. S.E.*, 23: 141–207. London: Hogarth.

Fudin, R. (1999). Subliminal psychodynamic activation: methodological problems and questions in Silverman's experiments. *Perceptual and Motor Skills*, *89*: 235–244.

Fulgencio, L. (2005). Freud's metapsychological speculations. *International Journal of Psycho-Analysis*, *86*: 99–123.

Galdston, I. (1956). Freud and romantic medicine. *Bulletin of the History of Medicine*, *30*: 489–507.

Gallagher, S., & Shear, J. (Eds.) (1999). *Models of the Self*. Thorverton: Imprint Academic.

Gardner, H. (1985). *Mind's New Science: A History of the Cognitive Revolution*. New York: Basic Books.

Gay, P. (1987). *A Godless Jew*. New Haven, CT: Yale University Press.

Gay, P. (1988). *Freud: A Life for Our Time*. London: Dent.

Gillett, E. (1996). Searle and the "deep unconscious". *Philosophy, Psychiatry, & Psychology*, *3*: 191–200.

Glaser, J., & Kihlstrom, J. F. (2005). Compensatory automaticity: unconscious volition is not an oxymoron. In: R. R. Hassin, J. S. Uleman, & J. A. Bargh (Eds.), *The New Unconscious* (pp. 171–195). Oxford: Oxford University Press.

Gomez, L. (2005). *The Freud Wars: An Introduction to the Philosophy of Psychoanalysis*. London: Routledge.

Gordon, R. M. (1986). Folk psychology as simulation. *Mind and Language*, *1*: 158–171. Reprinted in: G. Lycan (Ed.) (1990) *Mind and Cognition: An Anthology* (pp. 405–413). Oxford: Blackwell.

Greenwald, A. G. (1992). New look 3: unconscious cognition reclaimed. *American Psychologist*, *47*: 766–779.

Grimm, J. G., & Grimm, W. (1897). *Deutsches Wörterbuch*. Leipzig: Verlag von S. Hirzel.

Gundert, B. (2000). Soma and psyche in Hippocratic medicine. In: J. P. Wright & P. Potter (Eds.), *Psyche and Soma: Physicians and Metaphysicians on the Mind–Body Problem from Antiquity to Enlightenment* (pp. 14–35). Oxford: Oxford University Press.

Gusnard, D. A. (2005). Being a self: considerations from functional imaging. *Consciousness and Cognition*, *14*: 679–697.

Habermas, J. (1968). *Knowledge and Human Interest*. J. J. Shapiro (Trans.). London: Heinemann.

Hämeenniemi, E. (2007). *Tulevaisuuden musiikin historia*. Helsinki: Basam Books.

Hamilton, D. I., Katz, L. B., & Leirer, V. O. (1980). Organizational processes in impression formation. In: R. Hastie, T. M. Ostrom, F. B. Ebbesen, R. S. Wyer, D. L. Hamilton, & D. E. Carlston (Eds.), *Person*

Memory: The Cognitive Basis of Social Perception (pp. 121–154). Hillsdale, NJ: Lawrence Erlbaum.

Haskell, R. E. (2003). Is the unconscious "smart," or "dumb"? and if it's smart, how smart is it? One more time—with feeling. *Theoria et Historia Scientarium, 7*: 31–60.

Hassin, R. R., Uleman, J. S., & Bargh, J. A. (2005). *The New Unconscious.* Oxford: Oxford University Press.

Hatfield, G. (1992). Descartes' physiology and its relation to his pscyhology. In: J. Cottingham (Ed.), *The Cambridge Companion to Descartes* (pp. 335–370). Cambridge: Cambridge University Press.

Hodgkiss, P. (2001). *The Making of Modern Mind: The Surface of Consciousness in Social Thought.* London: The Athlone Press.

Holender, D. (1986). Semantic activation without conscious identification in dichotic listening, parafoveal vision, and visual masking: a survey and appraisal. *Behavioral and Brain Sciences, 9*: 1–66.

Holt, R. R. (1989). *Freud Reappraised: A Fresh look at Psychoanalytic Theory.* New York: Guilford.

Horgan, T. & Woodward, J. (1985). Folk psychology is here to stay. *Philosophical Review, 94*: 197–226. Reprinted in: G. Lycan (Ed.) (1990) *Mind and Cognition: An Anthology* (pp. 271–286). Oxford: Blackwell.

Jones, E. (1913). *Papers on Psycho-Analysis.* London: Bailliére, Tindall & Cox.

Kandel, E. (1999). Biology and the future of psychoanalysis: a new intellectual framework for psychiatry revisited. *The American Journal of Psychiatry, 156*(April): 505–524.

Kandel, E. (2005). *Psychiatry, Psychoanalysis, and the New Biology of Mind.* Washington, DC: American psychiatric Publishing.

Kihlstrom, J. F. (1987). The cognitive unconscious. *Science, 237*: 1445–1452.

Kihlstrom, J. F., Barnhardt, T. M., & Tataryn, D. J. (1992). The psychological unconscious: found, lost, and regained. *American Psychologist, 47*: 788–791.

Kihlstrom, J. F., Shames, V. A., & Dorfman, J. (1996). Intimations of memory and thought. In: L. M. Reder (Ed.), *Implicit Memory and Metacognition* (pp. 1–23). Hillsdale, NJ: Lawrence Erlbaum.

Kitcher, P. (1992). *Freud's Dream: A Complete Interdisciplinary Science of Mind.* London: MIT Press.

Kragh, H. (1999). *Quantum Generations: A History of Physics in the Twentieth Century.* New Haven, CT: Princeton University Press.

Kreiling, F. (1990). Leibnizian resonances. In: J.-C. Smith (Ed.), *Historical Foundations of Cognitive Science* (pp. 99–118). Dordrecht: Kluwer.

Kukla, A., & Walmsley, J. (2006). *Mind: A Historical & Philosophical Introduction to the Major Theories*. Indianapolis, IN: Hackett.

Kunst-Wilson, W. R., & Zajonc, R. B. (1980). Affective discrimination of stimuli that cannot be recognized. *Science, 207*: 557–558.

Laming, D. (2004). *Understanding Human Motivation: What Makes People Tick?* Malden, MA: Blackwell.

Laplanche, J., & Pontalis, J. B. (1973). *The Language of Psychoanalysis*. D. Nicholson-Smith (Trans.). London: Karnac.

LeDoux, J. (1998). *The Emotional Brain: The Mysterious Underpinnings of Emotional Life*. London: Phoenix.

Lennon, K. (1990). *Explaining Human Action*. La Salle: Open Court.

Levin, F. M. (1998). A brief history of analysis and cognitive neuroscience. *American Psychoanalyst, 32*: 26–27.

Libet, B. (1996). Neural processes in the production of conscious experience. In: M. Velmans (Ed.), *The Science of Consciousness: Psychological, Neuropsychological and Clinical Reviews* (pp. 96–117). London: Routledge.

Lindberg, D. C. (1992). *The Beginnings of Western Science: The European Scientific Tradition in Philosophical, Religious, and Institutional Context, 600 B.C. to A.D. 1450*. Chicago, IL: University of Chicago Press.

Lloyd, D. (1998). The Fables of Lucy R.: association and dissociation in neural networks. In: D. Stein (Ed.), *Connectionism and Psychopathology* (pp. 247–272). Cambridge: Cambridge University Press. http://www.trincoll.edu/~dlloyd/fablesof.htm

Looren de Jong, H. (2003). Causal and functional explanations. *Theory & Psychology, 13*: 291–317.

Macdonald, P. S. (2003). *History of the Concept of Mind: Speculations about Soul, Mind and Spirit from Homer to Hume*. Aldershot: Ashgate.

Macintyre, A. (2004). *The Unconscious. A Conceptual Analysis* (revised edn). Oxford: Routledge.

Mackie, J. (1965). Causes and conditions. *American Philosophical Quarterly, 2*: 245–255, 261–264. Reprinted in: M. J. Loux (Ed.), *Metaphysics: Contemporary Readings* (pp. 301–325). New York: Routledge, 2001.

Mancia, M. (2004). *Feeling the Words—Neuropsychoanalytic Understanding of Memory and the Unconscious*. J. Baggot (Trans.). London: Routledge.

Manson, N. C. (2003). Freud's own blend: functional analysis, idiographic explanation and the extension of ordinary psychology. *Proceedings of the Aristotelian Society, 103*: 179–195.

Marr, D. (1982). *Vision: A Computational Investigation into the Human Representation and Processing of Visual Information*. San Francisco, CA: W. H. Freeman.

Masson, M. E. J., & Graf, P. (1993). Introduction: looking back and into the future. In: P. Graf & M. E. J. Masson (Eds.), *Implicit Memory: New Directions in Cognition, Development, and Neuropsychology* (pp. 1–11). Hillsdale, NJ: Lawrence Erlbaum.

Matte Blanco, I. (1975). *The Unconscious as Infinite Sets*. London: Karnac.

Mayr, E. (1997). *This is Biology: The Science of the Living World*. Cambridge, MA: The Belknap Press of Harvard University Press.

McLaughlin, P. (2001). *What Functions Explain: Functional Explanation and Self-Producing Systems*. Cambridge: Cambridge University Press.

Mele, A. F. (2001). *Self-deception Unmasked*. Princeton, NJ: Princeton University Press.

Merikle, P. M. (2000). Subliminal perception. In: A. E. Kazdin (Ed.), *Encyclopedia of Psychology*, Vol. 7 (pp. 497–499). New York: Oxford University Press.

Morin, A. (2006). Levels of consciousness and self-awareness: a comparison and integration of various neurocognitive views. *Consciousness and Cognition, 15*: 358–371.

Moskowitz, G. B., Gollwitzer, P.M., Wasel, W., & Schaal, B. (1999). Preconscious control of stereotype activation through chronic egalitarian goals. *Journal of Personality and Social Psychology, 77*: 167–184.

Münsterberg, H. (1909). *Psychotherapy*. London: Adelphi Terrace.

Nagel, T. (1974). What is it like to be a bat? *Philosophical Review, 83*: 435–450.

Natsoulas, T. (2004). Vesa Talvitie & Juhani Ihanus's "On the nature of repressed contents". *Neuro-Psychoanalysis, 6*(1): 93–107.

O'Brien, G., & Jureidini, J. (2002). Dispensing with the dynamic unconscious. *Philosophy, Psychology, and Psychiatry, 9*: 141–153.

Palombo, S. R. (1994). Review of *The Rediscovery of the Mind*, by John Searle. *Psychoanalytic Books, 5*: 34–38.

Palombo, S. R. (1999). *The Emergent Ego: Complexity and Coevolution in the Psychoanalytic Process*. Madison, NY: International Universities Press.

Perkins, D. (2000). *The Eureka Effect: The Art and Logic of Breakthrough Thinking*. New York: W. W. Norton.

Piaget, J. (1973). The affective unconscious and the cognitive unconscious. *Journal of the American Psychoanalytic Association, 21*: 249–261.

Pötzl, O. (1917). Experimentell eregte Traumbilder in ihren beziehungen zum indirekten sehen. *Zeitschrift für die gesamte Neurologie und Psychiatrie, 37*: 3–4.

Power, M., & Brewin, C. R. (1991). From Freud to cognitive science: a contemporary account of the unconscious. *British Journal of Clinical Psychology*, 30: 289–310.

Pugh, G. (2002). Freud's "problem": Cognitive neuroscience & psychoanalysis working together on memory. *International Journal of Psychoanalysis*, 83: 1375–1394.

Reber, A. (1985). *The Penguin Dictionary of Psychology*. London: Penguin.

Rée, J. (1975). *Descartes*. New York: Pica.

Reinik, O. (1998). The analyst's subjectivity and the analyst's objectivity. *International Journal of Psychoanalysis*, 79: 487–497.

Ricoeur, P. (1970). *Freud and Philosophy: An Essay on Interpretation*. New York: Yale University Press.

Robinson, T. R. (2000). The defining features of mind–body dualism in the writings of Plato. In: J. P. Wright & P. Potter (Eds.), *Psyche and Soma: Physicians and Metaphysicians on the Mind–Body Problem from Antiquity to Enlightenment* (pp. 39–55). Oxford: Oxford University Press.

Rofé, Y. (2008). Does repression exist? Memory, pathogenic, unconscious and clinical evidence. *Review of General Psychology*, 12: 63–85.

Rubinstein, B. (1997). *Psychoanalysis and the Philosophy of Science. Collected Papers of Benjamin B. Rubinstein.* R. R. Holt (Ed.). Madison, NY: International Universities Press.

Rushing, R. A. (2006). Italo Svevo and Charlie Chaplin: dramatic irony and the psychoanalytic stance. *American Imago*, 63: 183–200.

Rycroft, C. (1968). *A Critical Dictionary of Psychoanalysis*. London: Penguin.

Ryle, A. (1949). *The Concept of Mind*. Harmondsworth: Penguin.

Salmon, W. C. (1989). *Four Decades of Scientific Explanation*. Minneapolis, MN: University of Minnesota Press.

Schacter, D. L. (1996). *Searching for Memory: The Brain, The Mind, and The Past*. New York: Basic Books.

Schafer, R. (1992). *Retelling A Life: Narration and Dialogue in Psychoanalysis*. New York: Basic Books.

Searle, J. R. (1992). *The Rediscovery of the Mind*. Cambridge, MA: MIT Press.

Searle, J. R. (1997). *The Mystery of Consciousness*. London: Granta.

Shanks, D. R., & St John, M. F. (1994). Characteristics of dissociable human learning systems. *Behavioral and Brain Sciences*, 17: 367–447.

Shevrin, H. (1990). Unconscious mental states do have an aspectual shape. Commentary/Searle. *Behavioral and Brain Sciences*, 13: 624–625.

Shevrin, H. (1997). Response to Solms. *Journal of the American Psychoanalytic Association, 45*: 746–752.

Shevrin, H. (2004). Commentary on "Freud's model of mind and functional imaging experiments". *Neuro-Psychoanalysis, 6*: 149–153.

Shevrin, H., Bond, J. A., Brakel, L. A. W., Hertel, R. K., & Williams, W. J. (1996). *Conscious and Unconscious Processes: Psychodynamic, Cognitive, and Neurophysiological Convergences.* New York: Guilford.

Shimamura, A. P. (1993). Neuropsychological analyses of implicit memory: history, methodology, and theoretical implications. In: P. Graf & M. E. J. Masson (Eds.), *Implicit Memory: New Directions in Cognition, Development, and Neuropsychology* (pp. 265–285). Hillsdale, NJ: Lawrence Erlbaum.

Shulman, R. G., & Reiser, M. F. (2004). Freud's model of mind and functional imaging experiments. *Neuro-Psychoanalysis, 6*: 133–141.

Shulman, R. G., & Rothman, D. L. (2000). Freud's theory of the mental and modern functional imaging experiments. In: J. Sandler, R. Michaels, & P. Fonagy (Eds.), *Changing Ideas in a Changing World: The Revolution in Psychoanalysis. Essays in Honour of Arnold Cooper* (pp. 163–169). London: Karnac.

Silverman, L. H. (1983). The subliminal psychodynamic activation method: overview and comprehensive listing of studies. In: J. Masling (Ed.), *Empirical Studies of Psychoanalytic Theories*, Vol. I (pp. 69–100). Hillsdale, NJ: Lawrence Erlbaum.

Silverman, L. H., Ross, D. L., Adler, J. M., & Lustig, D. A. (1978). Simple research paradigm for demonstrating subliminal psychodynamic activation: effects of oedipal stimuli on dart-throwing accuracy in college males. *Journal of Abnormal Psychology, 87*: 341–357.

Skokowski, P. (2003). Structural content: a naturalistic approach to implicit belief. *Philosophy of Science, 71*: 362–379.

Slavin, M. O., & Kriegman, D. (1992). *The Adaptive Design of the Human Psyche: Psychoanalysis, Evolutionary Biology, and the Therapeutic Process.* New York: Guilford.

Smith, D. L. (1999). *Freud's Philosophy of the Unconscious.* Dordrecht: Kluwer.

Smith, D. L. (2003a). Commentary on "On the nature of repressed contents". *Neuro-Psychoanalysis, 5*(2): 147–151.

Smith, D. L. (2003b). *Psychoanalysis in Focus.* London: Sage.

Solms, M. (1997). What is consciousness? *Journal of the American Psychoanalytic Association, 45*: 681–703.

Solms, M. (2006). Commentary on "The psychic apparatus, metapsychology, and neuroscience". *Neuro-Psychoanalysis, 8*: 99.

Spivey, M. (2006). *The Continuity of Mind*. Oxford: Oxford University Press.

Squire, L. R., & Kandel, E. R. (1999). *Memory: From Mind to Molecules*. New York: Scientific American Library.

Sulloway, F. J. (1979). *Freud, Biologist of the Mind: Beyond the Psychoanalytic Legend*. London: Burnett.

Sully, J. (1878). *Westminster Review*.

Tallis, F. (2002). *Hidden Minds: A History of the Unconscious*. New York: Arcade.

Talvitie, V. (2003). Repressed contents reconsidered: repressed contents and Dennett's intentional stance approach. *Theoria et Historia Scientiarum*, 2: 19–30.

Talvitie, V., & Ihanus, J. (2002). The repressed and implicit knowledge. *International Journal of Psychoanalysis, 83*: 1311–1323.

Talvitie, V., & Ihanus, J. (2003). On the nature of repressed contents—a working through of John Searle's critique. *Neuro-Psychoanalysis*, 5(2): 133–142.

Talvitie, V., & Ihanus, J. (2005). Biting the bullet: the nature of unconscious fantasy. *Theory & Psychology*, 15(October): 659–678.

Talvitie, V., & Ihanus, J. (2006). The psychic apparatus, metapsychology and neuroscience—toward biological (neuro)psychoanalysis. *Neuro-Psychoanalysis, 8*, 85–98.

Talvitie, V., & Tiitinen, H. (2006). From the repression of contents to the rules of the narrative) self: a present-day cognitive view to "The Freudian phenomenon" of repressed contents. *Psychology & Psychotherapy: Theory, Research and Practise*, 79(June): 165–181.

Tesser, A., Stapel, D. A., & Wood, J. V. (Eds.) (2002). *Self and Motivation: Emerging Psychological Perspectives*. Washington, DC: American Psychological Association.

Uleman, J. S. (2005). Introduction. In: R. R. Hassin, J. S. Uleman, & J. A. Bargh (Eds.), *The New Unconscious* (pp. 3–15). Oxford: Oxford University Press.

van der Eijk, P. J. (2000). Aristotle's psycho-physiological account of the soul–body relationship. In: J. P. Wright & P. Potter (Eds.), *Psyche and Soma: Physicians and Metaphysicians on the Mind–Body Problem from Antiquity to Enlightenment* (pp. 57–77). Oxford: Oxford University Press.

von Hartman, E. (1869). *The Philosophy of the Unconscious: Speculative Results According to the Inductive Method of Physical Science*. New York: Harcourt Brace, 1931.

von Schubert, G. H. (1814). *Die Symbolik des Traumes* (The Symbolism of Dreams). Bamberg: Carl Friedrich Kunz.

von Wright, G. (1998). *In the Shadow of Descartes: Essays in the Philosophy of Mind*. Dordrecht: Kluwer.

Wedin, M. V. (1988). *Mind and Imagination in Aristotle*. New Haven, CT: Yale University Press.

Wegner, D. M. (2002). *The Illusion of Conscious Will*. Cambridge, MA: MIT Press.

Weinberger, J. (2003). Commentary on "On the nature of repressed contents". *Neuro-Psychoanalysis, 5*(2): 152–153.

Weiner, B. (1992). *Human Motivation: Metaphors, Theories, and Research*. Newbury Park, CA: Sage.

Whyte, L. L. (1960). *The Unconscious before Freud*. London: Julian Friedman, 1978.

Wittgenstein, L. (1922). *Tractatus Logico-Philosophicus*. D. F. Pears & B. F. McGuinness (Trans.). New York: Humanities Press.

Wittgenstein, L. (1953). *Philosopical Investigations*. G. E. M. Anscombe (Trans.). New York: MacMillan.

Woody, J. M., & Phillips, J. (1995). Freud's "Project for a scientific psychology" after 100 years: the unconscious mind in the era of cognitive neuroscience. *Philosophy, Psychiatry, & Psychology, 2*: 123–134.

Wright, J. P., & Potter, P. (2000). Introduction. In: J. P. Wright & P. Potter (Eds.), *Psyche and Soma: Physicians and Metaphysicians on the Mind–Body Problem from Antiquity to Enlightenment* (pp. 1–11). Oxford: Oxford University Press.

Wright, L. (1973). Functions. *Philosophical Review, 82*: 139–168.

Young, A. W. (1994). Neuropsychology of awareness. In: A. Revonsuo & M. Kamppinen (Eds.), *Consciousness in Philosophy and Cognitive Neuroscience* (pp. 173–203). Hillsdale, NJ: Lawrence Erlbaum.

Yovell, Y. (2004). Commentary on "Freud's model of mind and functional imaging experiments". *Neuro-Psychoanalysis, 6*: 155–157.

Zaretsky, E. (2004). *Secrets of the Soul: A Social and Cultural History of Psychoanalysis*. New York: Vintage.

Žižek, S. (2006). *The Parallax View*. Cambridge: MIT Press.

INDEX